"Dumm

Trini

Trinity Mirror

C
Live

Business Development Director:
Mark Dickinson

Business Development Executive Editor:
Ken Rogers

Written by:
Walter Huntley

Design/production:
Vicky Andrews, Peter Grant, Zoë Egan

Illustrations:
Cathy Roberts/Peter Grant

Cover Design:
Trinity Mirror Book Team

Back Cover Picture:
Stephen Shakeshaft

ISBN 978-1-906802-03-5

SUPPORT FOR CHARITIES

Donations from Dummy Bullets' royalties are being made to the
Royal Artillery Charitable Fund (registered charity No.238197)
which for many years has provided care and support to ex-Gunners,
and to All Together Now (charity No.1106387) to help maintain
production of the free, inspirational magazine for disabled people
and carers, conceived and edited by former colleague, Tom Dowling,
himself disabled at the age of 20 after being shot by bandits.

DUMMY BULLETS

by

Walter Huntley

This book is dedicated to my long-suffering wife, Wendy, who could recite every word of it by heart and to Colonel IP Huntley, RM, who, I am immensely gratified to say, is still prepared to acknowledge me as his father.

CONTENTS

ABOUT THE AUTHOR

BORN in Liverpool in 1920, Walter Huntley developed an interest in ventriloquism as a schoolboy and found he had a natural flair.

He became a cub newspaper reporter the year before World War II broke out. Both strands to his life were to play a critical role in his extraordinary career with the Royal Artillery.

After being mobilised with the Territorial Army before the war and becoming a sergeant clerk, he stayed on after the end to fulfil a tour with his full size ventriloquial dummy, Gunner Jimmy Turner, as a member of the official British Army entertainment unit, popularly known as Stars in Battledress.

Entertainment became a virtual weapon of war when Britain was under threat of invasion by the Germans, and military chiefs saw it as vital to keep up morale. Huntley had become a clerk because few soldiers could do shorthand and typing. But his role as a ventriloquist, a top specialist act in variety, soon became even more important because the Army had even fewer ventriloquists!

He found himself being involved in troop show after troop show and touring military bases and civilian theatres particularly along the south coast under bombing, shelling, rocket attacks and flying bombs.

Huntley says: "The way it all worked out I never even saw a gun and spent most of the war talking to myself!"

After the demob, he returned to journalism on the Birkenhead Advertiser series, followed by a spell on the South London Observer and a return to Merseyside as a reporter with the Liverpool Daily Post and Echo where he eventually became associate editor of both newspapers.

FOREWORD

MY ventriloquist friend Walter has asked me to write the foreword to this book about our Second World War service together in Army troop entertainment. I'm really quite chuffed, but I wouldn't let on to him. Normally I'd call him Wal because it's easier to say than Walter, but I'd better give him the full works for this job. To hell with it, he's Wal.

Usually I had to say what he wanted me to say. But this time I'm going to say my bit on what it's like to be a ventriloquist's dummy. You get no pay. You've got no union and there's no minimum wage laid down or maximum working hours. As soon as you've done your stint you're shoved back into a trunk - or in my case an ammunition box. That's how I travelled from place to place on the Army's one-night show circuit. You've gotta be a contortionist as well as everything else.

No one comes up to you at the end of the night and says "Good show." Anything like that happened to Wal. He used to play an officer in our act. He'd have never made an officer even if they been handing out free commissions. It was the best joke in the act, not that it had much competition in Wal's script.

He likes to talk about us as "great pals". We got along all right but some of the things he got me to say made me look a real dummy.

Wal had his faults but in this book he tells it as it was. We were a small bit of history in a world war, a bit that's not been written about much because it was all part of the backdrop to the real show.

Finally, in case I've given you the wrong impression, it's not all bad being a ventriloquist's dummy. And it has one big advantage. Me and Wal have been together since that first troop show 70 years ago. He's now 88 and beginning to show it. I'm still 18.

Jimmy Turner

STOP PRESS!
SEPTEMBER 3, 1939
WAR IS DECLARED

AS events conspired to happen, I entered the Second World War on the Allied side in the spring of 1939. I was ahead of the actual declaration of war by more than five months because Bob, Doug and I had decided to get in there early.

It was really Bob who started it all. He was the editor of the Ellesmere Port Advertiser, a lively weekly paid-for newspaper in West Cheshire - this was long before free sheets. Ellesmere Port then was like a Wild West frontier town with verbal shootouts in the council chambers every meeting, a learning curve for an embryonic journalist.

At 24, Bob had trebled the circulation of the Advertiser. It may only have been from 1,000 to 3,000, but trebled none the less... His 24 years seemed an astonishingly advanced age to Doug and me, both still teenagers though we wouldn't have called ourselves that because the word was not yet in general use.

Bob, with the wisdom of his years, called us together one day in the 'Newsroom' - an area about the size of a large store cupboard and situated over a shop selling meat balls - and announced to us in earnest tones: "War is coming and we're all going to be involved. In the Great War (as the first one was still called) the biggest casualties were among the infantry and the lowest among the men of the heavy artillery.

"This is because it's well behind the lines and you just lob shells at the Germans who are much keener on the easier task of mowing down attacking infantry than trying to hit you.

"So what we do is this: we get trained on the big guns and become invaluable in that role and cosy through the war."

It seemed eminently sensible to Doug and me; even attractive given the likely option.

Bob later said that my reaction had mattered most because he felt that since I was the chief reporter - a position I held because I had joined the paper several months ahead of Doug - that my lead would be followed by Doug. As chief reporter I was being paid £1.30s a week (£1.50), a trivial amount by today's standards but a good wage for a cub reporter when a mature man could be expected to keep a family on £2.50 a week.

It was a straightforward decision for all of us. Our loyalty to our nation came before any loyalty to the Advertiser and our loyalty to personal survival came before that. But it has to be acknowledged with hindsight that no thought was given to what would happen to the paper, to which we had been so dedicated, when the war came and the entire editorial staff disappeared overnight to fight Hitler.

There was a major glitch when we discovered that all the TA heavy artillery units in our region had a full complement. Maybe Bob had not been so original in his thinking after all. However, the objective remained to avoid the infantry at all costs and we heard of a new horse artillery unit - the 149th Regiment RHA -

being formed at Hoylake, also then in Cheshire but now in Merseyside, and rushed over to enroll. Guns, even with horses, would still be better than the Poor Bloody Infantry and we could hardly have received a more welcoming enrolment than that conducted by BSM (Battery Sergeant Major) Hetherington whose geniality almost made one feel very much at home - and home the army was, indeed, going to be for more than six years!

Bob, now in zealous recruiting mode, had also persuaded his brother to enroll.

While all this was going on in this northwest corner of England, rather than planning to get more horses to wash down, the Germans were revving up their Panzers for Der Tag. Maybe no one of note at the War Office (after the war renamed the Ministry of Defence as a more acceptable title) had heard that the enemy was planning to use something called 'Blitzkrieg.'

There followed a few summer weekends of extraordinarily inept attempts to turn ourselves into signalers, the role to which we had been assigned. The operation was designed to set up field telephones which involved crawling on the stomach carrying huge coils of wire which ideally was to be fed across the countryside but instead insisted on coiling itself round the server, particularly in my case.

In a real situation all this had to be carried out under enemy fire. So much for blasting heavy artillery from well behind the lines. Nothing was going as predicted in the grand plan.

Except, of course, the war itself. Hitler did not disappoint. He invaded Poland on the Friday, the 1st of September, 1939, and Britain and France finally accepted that not even donating him huge swathes of Europe could buy peace. Anyway, there wasn't much more of Europe left to give him. War was declared on the Sunday.

I remember that Sunday well, which is surprising after what

had happened over the two days before. The Territorial Army was mobilised on the Friday and they actually thought of using the radio or, more accurately wireless, to spread the news that our King and Country needed us and we were to report to our bases.

Bob picked up Doug, Bert and me in his new Ford Prefect (£94 ex-works at Dagenham) and we rolled up at our base - if a field with a handful of hastily assembled Nissen huts qualifies for that description - to be greeted by a sergeant who announced: "I know you have been mobilised and told to come 'ere but we're not quite ready for you yet." I wonder if anyone had explained the situation to Hitler and asked if he could delay the war for a week or two. The sergeant continued: "Any of you who can go home do so and come back tomorrow." I don't think there was a soul left standing there 15 seconds later...

We jumped into Bob's car and roared off back towards our newspaper patch of Ellesmere Port and surrounding villages in the Wirral peninsula - three of us stopping off at The Woodland in upmarket Whitby. Probably simply saying we stopped there would be more accurate because it was dark by the time the three newly mobilised musketeers emerged to begin the journey to their homes. Bob, he of the lively mind further inspired by the output of a local brewery - no breathalyser then - said: "Let's have some fun as we go. We'll tell everyone there's a blackout test and they're to extinguish their lights and spend the rest of the night in the dark..."

And that's just what we did, along the New Chester Road, each taking a house some distance apart and telling the occupant that they were responsible for passing on the order to the next four houses either side. As we drove off, we had the satisfaction of seeing the lights go out one by one.

The amazing aspect of the whole affair was that we were all

dressed in such ill-fitting uniforms - including puttees that slipped down to look as if your boots were wearing collars - that it's a wonder the residents didn't just burst out laughing as soon as they opened the door. The puttees soon went as well as the canes with which we were issued in order to look smart in public and which involved 'stick drill.'

The next morning came a monumental hangover. This was not surprising because among my feats in The Woodland was to drink a large glass bowl full of bitter beer. It was normally used as a receptacle for Smith's potato crisps, the height of pub catering in those days. This I did for a wager which I won - the payment being a refill!

On newspapers then much more than now there was a drink culture, but not a binge culture as happened among youngsters in this century. I think it emanated from reporters on the dailies where, as I found later, you were always turning up at the wrong time to ask people questions they didn't want to answer; or you were the conveyor of bad news and there to see their reaction.

And always your story had to be over in time to catch the next edition and no mobile phones in my day. You needed a drink or several to be able to do the job!

My moment of truth came when I reported back to the regiment on that morning after mobilisation, a punitive and rapid sobering experience in which my heart sank till I felt it had reached my comfortable shoes, soon to be exchanged for ammunition boots and plimsolls. As we lined up for the indoctrination process I could see that those at the front end were being issued with, horror of all horrors, PT kit (now, no doubt, referred to as PE apparel).

Even more depressing was the man up a ladder working on the roof of one of the Nissen huts who was coughing almost incessantly with just the odd gasp of "Gas, first lot." We, of the second lot, were not under any illusions as were those naive young men of 1914 who enrolled enthusiastically that summer to fight a war that would be over by Christmas, only to be involved in four years of slaughter on a scale the world had never before experienced.

"There aren't enough Nissen huts built yet to take you all so we've had to make other arrangements," barked a sergeant major whose very appearance would have qualified him for a part in an Addams family TV series if there had been such a thing then.

But what was this - other arrangements? Home again to our own beds? The awakening was immediate. We were issued with a blanket each and escorted by a bombardier - corporal to the uninitiated in artillery parlance - to a large Victorian house, split into groups and each group allotted a bare room. This was where we would sleep.

The houses had been requisitioned at short notice. What happened to the families who had lived there remained a talking point among us. We never did find out because no one had been long enough in the army to dare to ask.

My room was in the basement with a concrete floor. I discovered that after a while even concrete seems to give to accommodate the contours of the body. We were sleeping nearly on top of one another and latecomers had a job persuading their way into a lie-down position.

It was all a dramatic change from home comforts but the young are resilient. The novelty, however, began to wear off by the time we were moved to iron beds in quickly erected huts.

That Sunday after war was declared we were summoned to a parade of the whole regiment to be addressed by our commanding officer, the much respected Lieutenant-Colonel Godfrey E Castle, MC who had served in the First World War and was looked on as the father of the regiment. His address went something like this: "So it's on and I want to assure you that it won't be long before we're over there again.

"We must train hard now for the task we are taking on. There may be a time of frustration ahead before we get there, but I promise you that you will get your chance of a crack at the Hun."

You will note that the enemy was not referred to as Germans or even Nazis, but 'the Hun' a demonising description much used in the First World War.

It was the crack at the Hun bit that worried me. I don't think I was alone in feeling more concerned at the crack the Hun might have at us.

ORDER OF THE BOOTS
READ ALL ABOUT IT!

FOR my years I was well informed and politically conscious, after all I was a newspaper man even if most of my scoops had been out of a glass, and I couldn't help feeling that the Hun had a pretty formidable army to be able to march into one country after another.

The Hun's Luftwaffe had also shown itself well skilled in dive-bombing and mass destruction in its role in the Spanish Civil War.

We usually called them Germans in those days rather than Nazis. That came later when they became our allies in NATO and it became fashionable to refer to the Nazis as if they were simply a Teutonic version of the Mafia and not much to do with Germans in general.

Churchill was an exception. He made great play of snarling out the word 'Nassi' when referring to Hitler and the other

German leaders.

That Sunday after the CO's rousing call to arms we were given what amounted to a virtual tutorial by Regimental Sergeant Major Smith whose initials were GG which seemed appropriate for the top NCO in a unit with horses, even though we hadn't yet got them.

The RSM addressed us as though we were totally devoid of the slightest inkling of how the British Army functioned which was pretty accurate in my case. He explained that life was governed by something called Part 1 Orders and Part 2 Orders, but it was the part one lot we needed to worry about.

They were posted - everything seemed to be 'posted' in the army including soldiers themselves as they were moved from unit to unit as though they were packed into Royal Mail bags each time - and the RSM emphasised that it was our duty to read Part 1 Orders every day on the board outside Regimental Headquarters.

They would tell us what our troop or battery would be engaged in and even name particular personnel for particular duties. Failure to read orders could lead to missing a parade and that would entail being put on a charge as would being improperly dressed and various other Transgressions, which he seemed to take some delight in listing. Put on a charge!

We didn't really know what that entailed but it sounded pretty awesome, not at all nice. That Sunday night while Bob and the others had slid off to the Punchbowl pub in Hoylake to join in a liquid community rendition of 'Roll Out The Barrel', 'South of The Border' and even old favourites like 'Pack Up Your Troubles' and 'Tipperary', I had to stay in barracks. The war was becoming no joke at all to find I was missing out on all fun or camaraderie to give it a more acceptable description.

I had been told by a lance-bombardier (half a corporal) that I was on PAD duty. "What's that?" I asked. "I dunno," he said. "I was just told to tell yer. Report to the battery office."

This I did and was issued with a bucket of sand and told to parade around and douse down any fires that I saw. Fires?

"Yes, fires," said the duty sergeant.

"Now the war's on the Germans could come over any time and drop incendiary bombs."

PAD turned out to be Passive Air Defence. I, and several others walking round with buckets of sand, were part of Britain's front line defence of Hoylake and the Wirral peninsula on that first day of World War II.

At the end of that first week I forgot to read orders and missed my first parade. I was fortunate enough to be hauled up before a battery sergeant-major of unusually benevolent disposition.

"There is one parade in the British Army that no one ever misses," he told me. "You managed to do it. It's pay parade. Be there next time." With that and "Dismiss," he handed me my pay packet. I was being paid. I was now a professional soldier!

The following week I got my first 24-hour pass and headed home to Bromborough, also then in Cheshire now in Merseyside. We had been told that we must all sharpen up and get our boots and buttons gleaming. I had put in some work on the buttons with Brasso and achieved satisfactory results - to me if no one else - but our boots were steeped in dubbin and resisted all attempts to obtain a shine.

There is always someone in a regiment who knows all the dodges and tricks of the trade. In our lot, it was Charlie, who, it was whispered in awe, had been a regular before joining the TA. Charlie was a small, wily looking character, scruffily dressed - not that I was entitled to criticise others on a matter of military appearance - who seemed to shuffle round in the shadows like a bookie's runner in the days before betting shops conferred legality on risking the housekeeping money on a horse.

Charlie had found himself in a position of some standing and influence among a crowd of rookies.

"What you do," he said, "when you get home you stick them in the oven and leave them there for a short while and this will help to take much of the dubbin out. Then you polish them up."

So I put them in the oven just like Charlie said. But I didn't leave them there for a short while like Charlie said.

In fact, I forgot all about them for hours; and when I opened the oven there was a sticky black mess which had been my boots with the toe and rear metal plates floating in it.

Panic! How do you go back to the army and explain that you have just destroyed the boots they gave you? We of the second lot had been brought up on stories of soldiers being blindfolded and shot for failing to turn up at their units.

What dire punishment was there for the heinous offence of turning up but without boots?

My father took command of the situation and told my elder sister, Gladys, to dash out and get to the shops quickly and buy me a pair of boots. It was Saturday and about 15 minutes before closing time. And in those days everything stayed closed from Saturday evening to Monday morning.

On Sunday, people paraded around in their best attire (hence 'Sunday best'), there was no public sport and little entertainment and the BBC played chamber music all day. No chance of getting any boots before Monday if she failed in her critical mission.

She made it in time and I received a pair of shiny black stylish civilian boots, extremely lightweight and unlike Army boots in almost every aspect. They were also a size too small. But I now had boots! They were so shiny that I spent the time before I had to go back trying to dull them down, the reverse of the antidubbin operation.

I tried to stick the metal plates on them but there was no such thing as Superglue in those days and they fell off as soon as I stood up. I realised the best I could do was to clump around making as much noise as possible every time my feet hit the ground. They were already pinching being a size too small and all this extra activity made them even less comfortable. But anything was better than being tied to a gun wheel or whatever.

Next day came the test when all my efforts at boot disguise could be exposed. As I stood lined up on parade and the officer moved ever nearer scrutinising each man closely I became even more apprehensive when he paid close attention to the appearance of the man next to me, particularly his boots.

"Get to work on those boots!" he snapped. "That's a damn poor show." Then there he was, eyeing me up and down.

"This is the first time I've seen boots like these," he said and as I prepared for the moment when I would be marched off under guard I heard him say "Get your boots like these," and I realised he was talking to the man next to me and pointing at my feet.

With that, he moved on and I rejoiced that I would see another dawn. Probably he was a recently recruited TA officer as green as most of us and wouldn't know ammunition boots from winkle-pickers.

I was getting tired, physically and mentally, of the effort of clumping around and in any event left with the problem that I would have to get official issue boots at some point. The opportunity came when it was announced in Part I orders that the Quartermaster Lieutenant, a gruff, formidable middle-aged man promoted from the ranks, would exchange any boots that had become badly worn or were giving trouble.

I judged the moment when the exchange, fortunately conducted by a QM's clerk not the QM himself, was at its height, slipped my boots among those being handed in and came away with the real McCoy. Another drama over.

I was told later that the clerk was called Danny Brabin who was embarking on a career in law and so was still probably more concerned with books than boots which is why I had got away with it. Brabin was soon sent off as officer material, served his country well and became Mr Justice Brabin.

So I can claim to have been served with a new pair of boots by a High Court Judge!

Another member of the 149th who achieved eminence was Captain (later Brigadier) Selwyn Lloyd, the regiment's first Adjutant who played a major role in the D-Day planning and a decade later was involved as Foreign Secretary in another war - the Suez crisis of 1956. He became Baron Selwyn-Lloyd of Wirral.

It was the caring Charlie who was instrumental in setting the initial course of my Army life which was to lead on to so much more. He seemed to feel that he had an obligation to take me under his wing and help steer me through the pitfalls which can besiege an innocent so singularly unsuited to the military environment.

I had been a few days on square bashing, including being the only one to turn left when the order from the sergeant was to right wheel - it caused some realignment among the squad and near apoplexy to the sergeant - when Charlie came sidling up one day and said: "They're looking for a batman."

Charlie always had his ear to the ground. He knew all the latest 'scandal' from the Officers' Mess.

"There's an officer who hasn't found a batman yet," he explained. "And it's a good job to have. Very few parades or drill."

Now that appealed. That really appealed.

So on Charlie's advice I defied the approach I had been given by an uncle "Never volunteer for anything," presented myself at the regimental office and timidly asked the sergeant if it was possible for me to be considered as a batman. "You really want the job?" he said with a note of incredulity. "It's sweeping and polishing and that sort of thing."

"Yes, I think I could do that," I said.

"You're a batman," he said.

The officer to whom I was assigned turned out to be extremely pleasant and, not at all demanding which was fortunate because under my service he was hardly the best turned out on the parade ground.

The Stanley Hotel at Hoylake had been requisitioned for the Officers' Mess with each officer having a room. There, I vacuum-cleaned, dusted, shined buttons and polished his Sam Browne (officer's belt) and generally tried my best to be useful to him.

I became particularly so after I discovered that he was a solicitor still trying to run his office in Liverpool. I told him I could do shorthand and typing and maybe he would like me to go home and get my Baby Empire portable typewriter and then I could do some of his office work for him right there within the regimental precinct.

He leapt at the idea and so started another surprising twist to my military career. He would dictate to me each morning before setting out on his Army duties and I would type up the letters ready for his signature later in the day.

SHOOTING FROM
THE LIP

SO life jogged on for a few weeks with the Sam Browne and vacuum cleaning coming a poor second to the steady office routine.

That, however, came to a sudden end when my officer was foolish enough, perhaps under the impetus of a few whiskies, to mention in the Officers' Mess, of his success in combining his military duties with still running his office.

I was told that word of the arrangement had reached the Colonel's ears and he had ordered that this shorthand-and-typing batman should immediately be moved to the regimental office as a clerk.

In the meantime, I had pretty well lost contact with Bob and the other two. Bob had been appointed Technical Sergeant - what exactly that entailed I don't know because I knew no one less technical. However he seemed to have found a niche for himself but had already upset the RSM by calling on his men to 'buckle to' when they were not responding quickly enough to his summons. He was made unmistakably aware there was no such thing in the Army as 'buckling to'.

Soldiers did things 'at the double'. He again upset RSM Smith when he sewed on his chevrons as a sergeant so wide apart, so high up his arm and in such an irregular pattern that his stripes looked like three boomerangs trying to fly off his uniform.

"What the hell are you doing with those?" bawled the RSM.

"You're in the Royal Artillery not the Royal Flying Corps."

RSM Smith was nearing the end of his service to his country and hadn't caught up on the mutation of the RFC into the RAF.

Now that I was in the regimental office I helped Bob in his secondary role as editor of the magazine of the 149th called Ubique Wherever - the Royal Artillery motto. It was an unambitious but effective form of production using stencils cut on a typewriter and then run off on a simple roller printer. It was sufficiently successful to sustain a price rise from 1d to 2d.

As I became further initiated into the Army it became clear to me the extent to which the Regimental Sergeant Major has a key role in any unit. He has been described as "the backbone of the British Army" because he is the central figure on whom the Commanding Officer relies to instill discipline, maintain standards and set an example of good soldiering. He is generally a figure to be respected and, in most cases, feared by the lower ranks and almost as much by the young officers.

Myself upsetting the RSM marked my debut in the regimental office. He sat in an area partitioned off from the general office within the hut. As the newest member of staff it was my duty to make the tea. I thought it was time we had a cup so I put the kettle on the portable gas ring.

There was a sudden bellow: "Get that thing off. The steam is ruining my buttons. Get it off at once."

I was told afterwards that tea was never made when the RSM was around because he complained that the steam took the shine off his buttons.

That was the trouble with the Army. People warned you afterwards about what you should never have done.

It wasn't much further into the war that all the shining came to an end. Someone at the War Office must have twigged that we were giving the enemy an unfair advantage (unfair to us) by making our troops so conspicuous. So off came all the brass buttons and on went Bakelite replacements.

I had another problem with the RSM.

After I arrived at Regimental Headquarters he had me in his office and told me: "I am the highest non-commissioned officer in the British Army. You always address me as Sir, but you never salute me. Is that clear?"

I replied smartly "Yes, Sir" and saluted equally smartly. His distorted face looked as if he could express no greater anger until he had painstakingly spelt it all out a second time only to be saluted a second time. I just couldn't stop my right arm from involuntarily shooting up.

That incident I think confirmed his view that his regiment had acquired a whole intake of congenital idiots of which I was the prime example. But the day came when he actually spoke to me in warm terms.

He had seen me perform my ventriloquial act at the first regimental troop concert staged in the parish hall. "I didn't think you had it in you lad," he said. "Very good. Dismiss."

I had begun my interest in ventriloquism as a schoolboy with a home made, flat-faced dummy on which I had constructed a primitive lever arrangement to provide moving lips. It all began after my father had been moved to London from Liverpool, where I was born, and I used to come to stay at my aunt's at the Mersey seaside town of New Brighton.

There, at the Floral Pavilion, was a show called Pleasure On Parade - they had ingenuous titles like that in those days - with a ventriloquist called Douglas Leonard, who inspired me to that DIY dummy. I heard of someone else who came from Liverpool who had also visited New Brighton and the Floral Pavilion to feed his theatrical ambitions many years before me and with much greater success - Tommy Handley.

He also had been a Service concert party entertainer in his case in the First World War. He developed the sketch 'The Disorderly Room' from his days in uniform and toured it round the halls before his fame in ITMA (It's That Man Again) on radio during the second war.

There was another link. The original Floral Pavilion has been rebuilt. It staged its last show in April 2007 with another great Liverpool comedian, Ken Dodd. Jimmy and I (I'll tell you all about him in a moment) were in a show with Ken in his early years when he was doing his 'Road to Mandalay' sketch.

Why do so many comedians come from Liverpool? Asked that question, Arthur Askey once replied: "because you have to be a comedian to live there." Only a Scouser himself could get away with a gag like that.

But to get back to the story of my boyhood venture into ventriloquism which was to play such a remarkable role in my life just a few years later...

The younger of my two sisters, Edna, generously bought me a small professional doll (Peter); I got another, a second hand one (Henry) and created a treble act, which I performed at friends' parties. I progressed, just before the war, to an over 4ft tall walking figure which I bought through Gamages in London for £12.10s (£12.50). I was told it had been made by a well-known maker called Quisto in Devon. It was this figure, Jimmy Turner, who was with me at those troop concerts in the Parish Hall in Hoylake.

Jimmy stayed with me at hundreds more shows, leading to my posting to the official British Army entertainment unit known as Stars in Battledress to be a full time entertainer in uniform. I had, in fact, been more or less in that role throughout my previous service!

But Stars in Battledress - aka the War Office Central Pool of Artistes - was yet to come. Jimmy Turner accompanied me in an ammunition box as I moved from unit to unit.

When the act developed into the routine where he was on a charge before me, with me sitting at a desk as an officer (a role I never came near to achieving in real life) an Army tailor measured up Jimmy and made a battledress for him which I have to this day - and Jimmy himself is still with me though our performing days are over.

Jimmy had what Gamages described as a "pneumatic mouth" which meant he could move his lips - an essential requirement in any dummy used in a vent act! He could spit, smoke, move his eyes, raise his top lip, move his arm and raise his eyebrows all for £12.50. For that first troop show I had billed him as "able to perform almost every human action."

That was the youthful journalistic streak breaking out and it caused so much ribaldry that I never used the description again!

I settled in well to the life in regimental HQ, was promoted to Bombardier acting Lance Sergeant and managed to avoid causing any more distress to the RSM.

We also put on several more parish hall concerts before the 149th regiment RHA moved to Rugeley in Staffordshire. Those parish hall concerts were very much homespun entertainment lacking the slickness of the more ambitious shows which developed later in the war, but they proved so popular with the civilian population that many of the troops couldn't get in even though the hall had been packed with extra seating and there were people standing several deep at the back.

Tickets had to be issued allowing a soldier one guest only! Entertainment was already showing its value as a wartime morale booster.

The acts which stay in my mind were Gunner Stan Hankin's rendition of 'Dreamin'oh my darlin love of thee' - a pinch from the odd odes repertoire of Cyril Fletcher, a well known comedian of the time; Battery Sergeant Major Connolly's lively piano interludes and Regimental Quarter Master Sergeant Charlie Rainford, in an old coat and with a scarf round his neck, telling us in full voice why "Murphy shall not sing tonight." He brought the house down.

The 149th RHA was still without the horses needed to justify its title. There was a rumour doing the rounds which I must make clear I never managed to verify that the CO, Second-in-command and Adjutant had all hired horses one day from a local farmer and endeavoured to ride them with discouraging prospects for their futures as mounted officers in charge of mobile guns.

They fell off one after another - or so the rumour had it.

True or false it caused much merriment and lightening of spirit among the servile lower ranks.

While we were at Rugeley I chummed up with Bob again - still had no contact with Doug - and we went out to a dance one night. It was a time when there had developed a form of hysteria over the possibility of the Germans dropping gas canisters on us and it was an order that we had our gasmasks with us at all times. Every so often there would be a gas drill. A whistle would blow and everyone had to don their masks which had to be carried even outside barracks.

When Bob and I were ready to return to the unit from the dance hall, where we had been happily bruising girls toes with our ammunition boots, we went to the cloakroom where we had hung our gasmasks to find only one there. Bob immediately pulled rank on me and said with a note of finality: "That's mine."

I was positive it belonged to me but he had been my editor and was still senior to me so I returned to base with proper boots this time, but no gasmask.

How do I get out of this one?

One of the lads in the office had somehow acquired an extra gasmask case which he generously loaned me. I filled this with a couple of half bricks and, as ordered, carried it at all times. The problem came when the gas alarm was sounded. You can't don a pair of half bricks. So I was constantly having to disappear into the latrines or hide away in the nearest convenient spot until the all clear was sounded - two blows of the whistle.

As with the boots I realized I had to face the music in the end. So I reported to the Quartermaster's Office and was told I would have to see the QM himself over this.

I had concocted some elaborate story to explain how I had lost it - to say I had left it hanging in a public hall would not have been well received - to which he simply said: "Really - and in what condition?" "It was a bit worn, Sir," I said. "It probably needed replacing," thinking things were going my way.

"I'm not asking about the gasmask, you bloody young fool, what condition were you in?"

"Perfectly sober, Sir" said I, for once telling it as it was.

Nothing more was said. He just threw another gasmask at me and waved me away wearily.

CASH CRISIS
CLUTCHING AT STRAWS

WE moved to a camp under canvas amid the Malvern Hills and it was here that I progressed from beer to raw cider. It was wonderful weather and I slept every night on a camp bed in the tent which was being used as the Colonel's office. Hot weather calls for much liquid and, totally unaware of the dynamite effect of raw cider, I obliged one evening in full measure.

I was out with a group of the lads and we returned to camp in extremely good spirits. That was the great plus of the sort of bonding drinking of those days - it produced bonhomie not aggression or any inclination to cause damage. In fact the unwritten rule was that you should be able to hold your drink.

It was not possible to go out drinking every night on a soldier's pay. It was usually once a week - pay night. I remember one occasion in mid-week when we were nearly all skint, and a bright spark suggested three of us should go out, buy a packet of straws and share a pint. He backed his proposal with a claim that drinking through a straw increased the intoxicant value of the beer. We tried it. It was totally ineffectual except to provide a good deal of laughter as we competed with one another to get the biggest intake and incapacitate the other straws.

There had been a lot of trench digging going on. That may have been to prepare us for our arrival in France - the Great War mentality still persisted - or just to give the lads something to do. It was, however, significant that the trenches surrounded the officers' area. First line of defence in case of invasion?

We were very late getting back to camp and had to move extremely quietly through the officers' lines to avoid being in trouble. So everything had to be done in a whisper. Suddenly I disappeared down into one of the trenches. I was so winded I had difficulty getting up let alone getting out and could hear the, whisper going round, "Where's Huntley?" Eventually I found enough breath to whisper back - in a whisper which was beginning to get beyond a whisper – "I'm down this trench."

The problem for the others was which trench and where. But they found me and began dragging me out. Then I slipped back again. All this commotion began to attract attention from the officers' tents. Torches began to go on and a voice rang out: "What's going on there?"

At this, we broke ranks and everyone stumbled forward in the dark through the officers' lines, tripping every so often over ropes and tent pegs, until we had reached the safety of our own tents as the noise of movement increased among the officers' tent.

Exhausted and with the cider now well fermented in my stomach I crashed into bed. Literally. It shot forward and sent articles from the Colonel's desk flying off into the dark. I subsided into a deep sleep, eventually waking momentarily and casting off most of my uniform. Dawn brought a scene to swiftly awaken the senses however dulled by alcohol.

Letters, files marked 'Most Secret', paper clips and ashtrays lay all mixed up with my underpants, vest, socks and other articles of my clothing. But the biggest worry of all was that an inkstand had toppled over and covered two letters in ink and dribbled down the front of the Colonel's desk.

I decided there was only way out of this new mess I had got myself into - tidy up quickly and destroy the ink splattered letters hoping their absence would not be noticed. Having returned the situation to something akin to normal I finished dressing but could not find my braces anywhere. Finally, I decided I would have to abandon the search as the Colonel could be turning up. The problem was that, without the braces, my trousers began gradually to fall down.

I counted on this being only a temporary situation until I could find some other form of suspension.

I was in the middle of a delicately chosen breakfast in the Sergeants' Mess with my head still performing gyrations when I was told: "The Colonel wants you."

I thought this time my Nemesis has come. The Colonel has discovered that two letters have disappeared off his desk and wants to know why.

I stood before him, my arms rigidly to my side to hold up my trousers - it was fortunate that as an NCO who was repeatedly in the CO's presence I was not required to salute each time on appearing before him - and awaited the damning question.

Instead, he said: "I have been irritated by what I thought was an insect flying around the tent and I kept warding it off without success. Eventually I turned to find this was the cause of the irritation to the back of my neck." It was my braces hanging from the main support pole to the tent. "I would be grateful, Sergeant, if you would remove this article of apparel."

I did so with abject apologies and retreated to restore myself to a comfortable situation. Nothing was ever said about the two missing letters. I long since gave up wearing braces and I have not drunk a drop of raw cider since that day. The episode took on the shape of a fashion note as the story was related among my confreres that "the Colonel was really tickled by Wally's braces!"

While all this was going on the 'Phoney War' - the early months where the land war consisted of a few skirmishes on the Western Front - had erupted into a very real war. Hitler, who had almost been thanked by our Prime Minister Neville Chamberlain for delaying hostilities and giving us more time to prepare (and did we need it!), had finally ordered his generals to launch the big offensive. The Panzer divisions swept across Europe with brutal efficiency and total disregard for the Geneva Convention on the rules of war. They dive bombed columns of civilian refugees, executed prisoners of war, including some British, destroyed and killed anything and anyone at random.

Survivors of the evacuation through Dunkirk of the BEF (British Expeditionary Force) began arriving at our camp.

I talked with them and made notes. They had horrific stories to tell. The Phoney War was definitely over; the Germans had begun total war and despite the evacuation success we had lost our best military equipment.

The reaction in this country saw a strange dichotomy. There were those who stoically accepted what was happening and others who foresaw that this country was in greater peril than any time since the Roman invasion. Not even Napoleon posed such a threat. We were alone, totally alone.

As Sergeant Tommy Rourke, the 149 PT instructor, put it "Now we're Kelly's eye" - Number One in Army housey housey language (Bingo). Sergeant-Major Turner (no relation to Jimmy!) added: "Yes, and we've nothing left to defend ourselves with but junk."

The Germans had used many sympathisers and agents in their sweep across Europe to serve them as spies - the Fifth Column as it was dubbed. As this became known it fed a degree of paranoia in this country. Parachutists were being spotted on a fairly regular basis - we had a report of a landing near the camp but by the time our search party had been mobilised and reached the area if any parachutist had been there he would have had time to be back in Berlin.

Even neighbours of long standing could become suspect, especially if they had a chink in their curtains which moved erratically in the breeze and emitted a light through the blackout. Could dear old Mrs. Annie Tomlinson be a German agent sending messages? She had once said she didn't think Hitler "was too bad."

In the 149th magazine Ubique we had carried warnings about not giving information to strangers particularly on the strength of the regiment. One reader facetiously pointed out that a shop in Hoylake had in its window the picture of the entire regiment taken in the September war was declared and all a spy had to do was to count the bodies in the picture.

The Government PR teams also contributed to the general air of caution. Their bright lads had a field day with posters declaring Walls Have Ears, Keep It Under Your Hat, Careless Talk Costs Lives and one that would later have had feminists fuming: Be Like Dad - Keep Mum.

It was against this background that when a policeman turned up at 149 Regiment wanting information about the regiment I tried to contact the Adjutant.

The duty officer, a young lieutenant, came over to the office and said the Adjutant was off camp but he would deal with the policeman. The constable, who had produced his identity card, said he had several important questions to ask - how many rifles have you got, how well trained are you, what is your full strength? And several more.

The young officer obtained all the information he had asked for and away went the PC.

I was only 19 myself but I was uneasy. I probably had more street cred than the lieutenant having witnessed a parade of the seamy side of life during my court reporting experience. This was also in an era when there was still a deeply ingrained respect for authority - and no one represented authority more than a policeman.

As a precaution I took the policeman's number - 506 - and as soon as the Adjutant was on camp again I reported what had happened to him.

To say he was alarmed would be an understatement. "Get a rifle and ammunition and I'll get a car," he rapped... "We've got to chase after this blighter."

We caught up with him walking jauntily a couple of miles down a Worcestershire country road. The Adjutant gave him a thorough grilling. He explained that he was simply collecting information for a return the Chief Constable had to make on the forces in his area.

Even in war bureaucracy still flourishes! Since units were constantly on the move it was difficult to understand what use such area by area information could be - except perhaps to the Germans if they did invade.

Mind you it seemed that the Germans already knew a good deal about the disposition of our units in the UK if you believed the propaganda from Germany of the Nazi collaborator William Joyce, better known as 'Lord Haw Haw.'

In one broadcast he said that a number of units had moved into Staffordshire and he singled out the 149th regiment even giving the composition of the advance party.

It was clever stuff; a few genuine facts like this and people began to believe everything he said. But how did he know so much about the 149th? It was a chilling warning that all those posters on security were not there just for a laugh.

After the war, Joyce was captured and executed for treason.

Going back to the policeman's visit, the Adjutant said: "You were absolutely right, Sergeant, to act as you did. I'll mention it to the CO."

There and then I began to see myself as having released a latent talent which could make me an invaluable asset to the nation's counter-espionage service. Had I not spotted what could have been a bogus policeman (even though he wasn't) when a commissioned officer had singularly failed to do so?

Had I not gained a credit in French in the School Certificate exam at Wirral Grammar School? Was all this to be wasted at a time when my country's need was so desperate?

Bob and Bert had both been posted to other units, I had lost all contact with Doug and I had begun to ponder on my own future. I decided there and then to act - and went back to the office to type out my application for a transfer to the Army Intelligence Corps.

That should get things moving.

It did - ME!

GET THE SHOWS ON THE ROAD

I WAS posted. But not to the Intelligence Corps.

Obviously it was not considered that I would be a great loss to the 149th because my request was promptly forwarded up the line and, without any explanation, I was sent to serve at 3rd Corps HQ in Shropshire.

Maybe the assessment of my future prospects was influenced by an error I made in typing out a letter from the Colonel to the General Officer Commanding Western Command proposing Knutsford, an up market Cheshire town, as a suitable place to hold a proposed conference. Regretably, I managed to transpose the order of the letters 'n' and 'u' with a result I leave you to work out.

Fortunately, the General had a sense of humour and asked in his reply for further details on the services offered at Knutsford.

The reply totally baffled the Colonel and Adjutant who at first failed to study the original letter. On re-examination, the penny dropped and I heard howls of laughter from the Colonel's office.

I was then called in to share in the joke at the same time being told to be more careful in future because I could be handling communications where errors could lead to catastrophic results.

Maybe the Colonel remembered the famous story of how a communication went wrong in the First World War, no doubt apocryphal. The message to be sent down the line was "We are going to advance, please send reinforcements," and finished up at point of receipt as "We are going to a dance, please send three and four pence."

Whatever the reason, I was on my way. My posting to 3rd Corps HQ meant saying goodbye to the lads of the 149th which was turned into an anti-tank unit and saw distinguished service with the Eighth Army in the Western Desert under General Montgomery gaining four DSOs, two MBEs, 10 MCs, three DCMs, seven MMs, a British Empire medal and 22 mentions in dispatches.

It was Montgomery who first inspired in me the thought that we really did have a chance of winning the war with his little rasping voice on the radio in 1942 declaring that we were going to "knock the enemy for six". I had never heard anyone speak before with such credible confidence, particularly since morale had been eroded to zero after Prime Minister Neville Chamberlain's boast "Hitler has missed the bus in Norway," just before the Germans threw us out of Scandinavia.

Montgomery had just taken over command in Egypt and he went on to do what he promised at El Alamein. Monty was like Churchill just what you need in war - a showman who can also deliver. Victory at Alamein altered the mood of the country.

I remained baffled why a request to join the Intelligence

Service should lead to a posting as a clerk to Headquarters, 3rd Corps, at Whitchurch, which in any case was run by RASC (Royal Army Service Corps)clerks and nothing to do with the RA Third Corps who had just returned from France, battered and bruised after the BEF retreat.

Maybe they were short of a clerk or it had been decided that I could be better kept under surveillance there on the odd chance that I might actually be considered suitable for intelligence work. The Army, like the Almighty, moves in mysterious ways. But if it was for the latter reason I obviously failed the test because after several months I was posted again, this time to the RA Depot, Woolwich, London, again without being given any reason. But while I was at Whitchurch Jimmy Turner and I were once more called upon to tread the boards, as taking part in variety was known.

During the latter part of 1940, the year The Few in their Spitfires and Hurricanes beat off the Luftwaffe and showed how empty was Goering's boast of quickly gaining air superiority, there had developed a recognition at the highest level of the need to maintain morale in what had become a virtual siege situation.

The threat of invasion was very real and we were very weak. We had lost a huge amount of military equipment in the retreat from France and left behind some of our best regular troops. Minds must not be left to dwell on our plight.

In this context, entertainment of the population had by now become an important consideration, almost a weapon of war.

Many well-known professional artistes gave their services in entertaining the troops - including comedian Tommy Trinder, George Formby with his ukulele and the girl singer who became the Forces' sweetheart and the favourite of them all, now Dame Vera Lynn.

The War Office, however, felt the forces must also do their bit and began to encourage units to form concert parties to provide garrison entertainment and extend it to the public.

The Daily Mirror, welcoming the move, commented: "Today there is probably more real talent in uniform than there is out of it and these garrison theatres are certain to provide some of the stars of the peacetime stage of tomorrow.

"The grant to equip the theatres will be money well spent for it will add to the contentment of the serving men."

No mention of women at this time but they were to play a big part in Service shows.

In the part of England where I was stationed, Western Command, no doubt in common with other regions, set about putting on as many shows as possible. In 3rd Corps the matter was taken so seriously that the formation of a Corps concert party was put under the personal supervision of a brigadier no less - Brigadier Lorie, with Captain DA Clarke-Smith, a distinguished Shakespearean actor and now Entertainments Officer, Western Command, as the producer.

I had been there only four days and had not had time to have Jimmy sent to me by rail in his ammunition box. Being the only ventriloquist that 3rd Corps was ever likely to have I was put in a car and dispatched to my home in Bromborough, Wirral, to collect him.

Surprisingly, I found rural Whitchurch had an historic war background. It was the scene of two battles in the English Civil War, first being taken by Cromwell's Parliamentary forces in 1643 and then being retaken by the Royalists under Prince Rupert the following year.

Three centuries later it was the scene of another battle between two military adversaries conducting operations on their home ground. This time it was not over the future of

England but the future of a concert party. The Brigadier had decided to entrust Major W Parkes, MC with the duty of ensuring that the 3rd Corps concert party should be set up speedily and be able to give a performance of the highest possible standard. This may have resulted from news being received that the GOC-in-C Home Forces was planning to attend the opening night.

My notes show that Clarke-Smith seemed to resent this arrangement, made, I think, because the Captain, a brilliant actor, could be less than punctilious in organisation. The result was a distinctly uncivil conflict with the Major over almost every aspect of the show - from the auditions onwards.

Again, my career took an unexpected twist. I was not even a senior NCO - I was a Bombardier Acting Lance Sergeant and unofficial assistant producer - and I found myself being courted by both sides seeking to find out what the other had been saying and doing.

All the artistes were fulltime and I recorded in my notes: "No effort is spared to make it a real success. Costumes, scenery, props - anything you want you just ask for it."

All should have gone well – it didn't. One major problem was an apache dance number between a burly lance-corporal and an ATS girl he had to throw to the ground, twirl around and kick as she lay there - a part of the act he was embracing with worrying enthusiasm. Added to this, he kept turning up clearly the worse for a few drinks and the poor girl was becoming very apprehensive at the whole idea. It took a great deal of argument and appeals to her commitment to the adage that the show must go on to persuade her to go on with it!

The dress rehearsal was a shambles with the Corps Commander, Lieutenant General Anderson and Brigadier Lorrie looking on. Now involved were a general, a brigadier, a major, a captain and an assortment of other ranks with the General Officer Commanding waiting in the wings to pass judgment. Viewed with the hindsight of some 70 years, that may seem a formidable array of military expertise to set up a concert party; but that's how it was in those dark days of 1940 in the effort to keep up the nation's spirits.

At this point, the Brigadier himself took over, rearranged the running order and chopped a couple of acts. The finale was rewritten with Jimmy and me closing the show with Jimmy singing a patriotic number 'Thumbs Up' and the rest of the cast assembled behind us and coming in on the chorus.

We did two shows with The Fig Leaves - as the concert party was called - and Jimmy and I took part in a number of charity shows including a performance in the town hall at Whitchurch in aid of the British Legion with civilian artistes including Adrienne Allen and Ronald Squire, well known actors, and Harry Mortimer, famed cornet soloist of Foden's Band and the Halle Orchestra.

It was at Whitchurch that Jimmy gained his independence - he was enabled to perform some distance from me. Through the various charity shows for civilians in which we took part I had become friendly with Maurice Wright, of the town's Regent Cinema, and had told him of my ambition to be able to work Jimmy by remote control.

His operator, John Jones, became interested in the idea and spent hours devising and making a cable wire and air pump control system with simple one hand control. I was immensely grateful to him and began to develop my act to a new level.

Then the war intervened again.

Someone further up the line had presumably discovered that a Royal Artillery bombardier clerk (acting lance sergeant) had somehow found his way into a headquarters staffed by RASC clerical personnel and decided it was time he was back with the RA.

Captain Clarke-Smith said he felt sure the Brigadier would be able to have the order rescinded so I could stay with the show. But it was not to be. I left 3rd Corps with a note from Clarke-Smith to the Entertainments Officer, RA Depot: "Sergeant Huntley was a valuable member of our concert party and is an extremely able and amusing ventriloquist. We are sorry to lose him but know you will find him useful and appreciate his turn as much as we did."

During my time with 3rd Corps I was billeted with a civilian family and taken on a trip to see the shell crater left by a German bomb which had blown off the leg of a cow. It was the most exciting moment Whitchurch had ever experienced. I went from that rural scene to Woolwich at the height of the nightly, all-night blitz. And, literally, struggling to survive.

It was November 1940 when I arrived at Euston Station to make my way to Woolwich. I had a rail warrant but I was soon told by a rail official "There are no trains to Woolwich, mate. The line's down." There was I, kitbag, rifle and full rigout and a useless rail warrant. My last money was a ten shilling note, a hell of a lot to a young soldier at that time.

I weighed up the few drivers in the taxi rank and picked out the one who looked the most amiable. "Any chance of getting me to the artillery depot at Woolwich for ten shillings?" I asked.

"Yeah. I'll do that," he said. "Hop in." I didn't take taxis in those days so I don't know whether he did me a favour or just did me. The devastation I saw as we drove there was mind numbing.

Coming from another part of the country hardly touched by war brought the stark reality of what this part of England was going through. Other cities had their blitzes, but only London went through such a sustained and ferocious level of attack.

STRUCK DOWN BY *GERMAN* MEASLES!

NIGHT after night, the sirens wailed their frantic warning, often even before it was really dark, to alert everyone that the bombers were on their way. It would be hours before the calming, even noise of the 'all-clear' would bring some relief.

Woolwich Barracks was the most impersonal base at which I was stationed. It was so vast and, being used as a transit camp, was packed with soldiers coming and going.

With the long nights, the bombing and total blackout there was only an extremely limited time at the height of the blitz when any attempt could be made to achieve even a state of organised chaos.

The barracks itself was being hit - I was told many of the records of the men there had been destroyed when one of the offices was badly damaged - and the only way to find out exactly who was "present and correct" was to order a total parade of everyone. While officers went round searching the toilets, out buildings and any crevice or crack where a human being could conceivably hide, the rest were forming up on the parade ground being joined all the time by the stragglers, some of whom had been flushed out. They were formed up separately from the rest of us.

Officers then went round taking the details of every soldier - name, rank, number, what job they were doing at the barracks or if they had not been assigned any job when they had arrived and from which unit.

Amid all the chaos and confusion there were some men who had a very good sideline - not in the RA Depot but down at the Arsenal making the means of war for which they were paid the going rate as civilians. They only visited the depot to check in as soldiers on pay parades.

So they weren't hiding in the toilets or anywhere else. They were there in person because the big parade had been set on a pay parade day to catch them out. It put an abrupt end to the double life and double pay routine.

I was fortunate. My status was totally legit. After a few weeks of just attending morning parade and then loafing about I had been appointed sergeant clerk at the Courts Martial Office.

The charming and dashing Lieutenant Lawrence Firmin of the blonde hair and blonde moustache was the Courts Martial Officer. I think he came from Maidenhead and seemed top drawer, but without any side. I'm sure he would have been immensely attractive to the ladies. He was always relaxed but efficient and we got on extremely well. I often think of him now and wonder if he survived the war.

During the four months I was in the Courts Martial Office we handled 87 cases. One of the most interesting jobs I had was to interview and take a statement from a young soldier who was being held in custody at Orpington having been going the rounds of units in Kent and Sussex posing as an officer and enjoying the comforts of mess life.

He had somehow acquired a subaltern's uniform and would just present himself to the adjutant of the unit he had chosen to visit and express considerable astonishment when told that they knew nothing off him.

His answer was that he had been told his papers would be dispatched in a day or so but to report in the meantime. This gave him several days grace until he was told the regimental office would 'chase up' his papers. He then took off to work his scam on another unit.

Inevitably, he was eventually going to be exposed as a fraud. But he had the utmost bad luck. By a million to one chance an officer from one of the units where he had carried out his deception was posted to the unit where he had just 'posted' himself and recognised him. He was a lad who was confident and articulate and seemed to be well educated.

I asked him why he did it and he replied: "It was just something to do." I pointed out he was certain to be caught out and he said he realised that, but he didn't care.

I don't know what happened to him. After serving his time in detention, a young soldier of such free spirit and enterprise could well have gone on to win a medal. The most surprising things can happen in war.

There is also a distorted disregard of the value of life at a time when multiple death is a daily fact. One night, a landmine landed close to the barracks. The buzz was that two sentries on duty simply disappeared like most of the street nearby.

Even though many people would have been in their shelters, some no doubt died in the houses which had been reduced to rubble.

There was genuine anguish among the ranks at the destruction caused by the landmine which reflected a special venom towards the Germans. It can be summed up in four words: "Our chip shop's gone."

'Going sick' was a dodge practised by many old sweats when they felt like a rest from duties. Those who became really practised at the art would progress from 'excused boots' to being granted an appearance before a medical board in an ambitious effort to secure a discharge from the Service.

I remember the story of one soldier at 3rd Corps who suddenly reported, to the astonishment of those serving alongside him, that he had become virtually lame and was so persistent in claiming he was not fit to serve any longer that he was finally sent before a board. He was with a group of others on a similar quest waiting outside the building where the hearing was taking place when someone produced a football.

Now he had been a keen amateur footballer and was quickly involved in showing the others how good he was. In no time, he had scored a goal between the makeshift goalposts.

He was just in time before he was summoned to appear before the board. As soon as his name was called, he limped off to face judgment. Unfortunately for him, the chairman of the board had just glanced out of the window and spotted him in his moment of triumph. Not surprisingly he was turned down. As he left the room, still limping, the chairman said: "you don't need to keep that up any more." It was an own goal with personal consequences as hard to bear as if he'd been playing in the Premiership.

Not many tried anything on at Woolwich. The procedure there was that before reporting to the Medical Officer you had to hand in your palliasse and blankets at the QM store.

The thinking behind this was apparently that you would then

be ready to be sent to hospital if it was felt that you needed a proper check-up.

It is very difficult for any doctor to detect whether "me back's hurting me, Sir" is genuine or not so many would simply prescribe "a day's rest on the bed and if it's still bad report back tomorrow."

The immediate problem for the 'patient', who had probably spent some time in the line waiting for attention, was that he had no bed because apart from the iron bed frame it had all been handed in to the QM's office.

So it was round there again to collect his palliasse and blankets - not necessarily the ones he had handed in - and by that time if he was genuinely sick he would be even worse and would merit treatment next day. Contrarily, if he was just trying it on he would probably decide that there was less fatigue in doing fatigues than going through this again.

I was fortunate that I never had to go sick at Woolwich. In fact, the only time I received hospital treatment was in February1940. Several of us from 149th Regiment, still at Hoylake, were admitted to Clatterbridge Hospital, Wirral, suffering from - of all things - German measles. It was a situation which occasioned much merriment. The disease itself had hardly any effect and the suffering involved was occasioned by the young nurses, then, of course, all female, as they passed from one bed to another on which lay lusty young soldiers feeling not the slightest bit ill.

The 149th regiment was formed of volunteers, apart from the regular core staff, mostly from the Wirral peninsula. Some came from Wallasey, Wirral and Calday Grammar Schools, but whatever their schools most shared much the same sort of background. Once you moved on to other units you entered a widely based, largely conscripted society. The British Army had become very different from the peacetime army staffed by regulars. The one thread in common with most of us was that we had been taken from our normal life pattern - our comfort zone - and plunged into a wholly foreign environment with its own arcane rules of which we knew very little and the learning process could be painful.

It was at Woolwich Depot that my showbiz streak came to my rescue in a desperate situation. The RSM had decided to issue a stark reminder that it was a military establishment. He suddenly called an early morning parade with an NCO visiting every barrack room with the stark shout "On parade!"

Bleary-eyed soldiers shuffled on to the parade ground from all directions and formed up on the long stretch of area in front of the main building. I was by then a lance-sergeant.

"Senior NCO present step forward," barked the RSM. I looked around and could see no one else with three stripes, but had learned enough not to step forward. I had, however, made enough movement among the rigid ranks to attract the RSM's attention.

"That sergeant, there," he shouted. "You're the senior NCO present, aren't you?" "Yes, Sir" I said as one does in such circumstances, despite the fact that they were probably many senior to me.

"Well you do as you're ordered then, don't you, and step forward?" Another "Yes, Sir" and there I was out there at the front, my back to the men and facing the RSM on the British Army's longest parade ground in the United Kingdom.

"Fall out all other senior NCOs," barked the RSM. He had got his victim. There was a stamping of feet as the escapees departed.

"Now, Sergeant, I want you to take this lot on a march through the town." His voice boomed out around the parade ground...

GUNFLASHES!

Bring on the girls... Gunflashes was one of the first Army concert parties to include an ATS chorus and individual female artistes.

A.T.S. "Gunflashes" Make Up

These A.T.S. girls, making up to give a show for the Forces, are members of the Royal Artillery Depot concert party. They call the show "Gunflashes."

Gunner Jack
Cardew with
Hutton and
Hicks

Hicks and
Hilton
perform their
cross-talk act.

"GUNFLASHES" DANCE NUMBER JACK CARDEW & DOREEN SWAN

to your friend
Jack
_8/6/41._

Jack Cardew and his dancing
partner. Jack produced
Gunflashes, the RA Depot
Concert Party, and became a
great friend and mentor.

GUN-TOWN CHANGES ITS MIND

And the Gunners Like Dover Pride

Express Staff Reporter

DOVER , Friday - The gunners of Hellfire Corner who sank that German supply ship in the dark of Thursday morning, have changed their local status from Public Grouse No. 2 (after the weather) to Public Heroes No. 1.

News of the sinking and Mr. Churchill's telegram "Hearty congratulations on the good shooting of the Dover guns" have done that, partly because of the success, more because a specific target was revealed.

Those in Dover who thought the guns shot up the French coast for the fun of it have groaned at the shelling alerts and muttered "Those so-and-so gunners" as they stumbled to the shelter.

They knew there would be retaliation from the French coast. That smashed supply ship which tried to sneak through the Straits has changed it all. The townsfolk think the gunners are long-suffering, hardy men. The gunners think the town has done fine to stand the shelling with only a few grumbles. Dover does carry on through it all, dourly and calmly. It is something you could call Dover Pride.

They Took to the Caves

When a shelling alert sounded, many in the Dover area headed for the famous white cliffs where they had made themselves a home from home in the caves.. They took food, often fish and chips bought on the way, and had stoves there so they could brew up. Whist was a popular way of passing the time till the all-clear sounded..

Others went down to the basements, garden shelters or dugouts or to the public shelters. In this town the arrangement was men in one shelter so they could smoke and women in another so they could do their darning or knitting - and, of course, make tea. When the guns fired they rocked the area around them sending glasses and cups flying in the officers' and sergeants' messes.

The night after the German supply ship was sunk Dover guns engaged another enemy ship and the alert sounded again. The chief Civil Defence Officer announced over the town's amplifiers: "HM Forces must return to their stations or barracks or proceed to the nearest shelter"

The warning was shown in cinemas and announced from the stage of the local theatre. Most public houses closed, but the crypt at the Shakespeare Head stayed open. An impromptu party there to celebrate the "kill" of that morning had to be delayed and half-drunk glasses abandoned.

The Royal Artillery log book recorded the sinking in the following clinical record:

```
0435: Alarm sounded
0507 First round fired
0742 Last round fired
0850 All clear
About 80 rounds fired
```

The Sketch

"THE GUNFLASHES" spelt out their topical cast-name at the finale of their excellent show.

An A.T.S. high-kick during the dancing turn "We All Smile Again," by VOLUNTEERS YVONNE GLOVER, DOREEN SWAN, and RITA COUSINS.

"Rhythm Interlude," with GUNNER FA|LCE.-BOMBARDIER BAVIN, and GUN| CARDEW at the "mike."

|R ELAINE SEARL sang into the microphone.

|ancing in "Waltz-Time" are VOLUN-|ER DOREEN SWAN and GUNNER CARDEW.

CALLING themselves "The Gunflashes," A.T.S. Volunteers and members of the R.A. put on a very successful joint show at a Royal Artillery depôt by Bombardier Hicks and Gunner Cardew. Captain Winn, R.A., was the organiser, and Bombardier Hicks and Gunner Cardew arranged the numbers; and members of the cast built the scenery themselves from bombed wood, after a raid at their own barracks.

"A GUITAR AND SPAIN" is the fourth item on a programme which consisted of twenty-five numbers and played to packed and enthusiastic houses of its own comrades-in-arms.

Walter Huntley with Porky
and his guitar.

With Best Wishes for a Happy
Christmas and New Year from

WAL HUNTLEY

and

" Jimmy
Turner "

Still 'GOING PLACES' with
'STARS IN BATTLEDRESS'

WAL. HUNTLEY

Alone this time: Woolwich, the British
Army's longest parade ground in the
United Kingdom, where Walter
Huntley gave the best show of his life.

Treading the Boards

Walter finally mustered 38
figures but Jimmy Turner
remained his best mate.

A NIGHT OF NIGHTS

REGIMENTAL CONCERT

PARISH HALL, HOYLAKE   THURSDAY NIGHT, 19.30 HOURS

SGT-MAJ. CHAB. RAINFORD

THE POPULAR ENTERTAINER IN HIS LATEST ACT.

B.S.M. C.V. CONNOLLY

THE FRIEND OF TOTTERING TODDLERS A NEW NOVELTY

BDR. WALTER

WITH A BRAND NEW VENTRILOQUIAL ACT
PERFORMED ALMOST

TONIGHT

L/BDR.
("DREAMIN' OF THE ...)
HANK ... ... R. KING

COMEDY ...

W. WOODS

COMEDIAN FEATURING SOME OF THE "HITS" OF
THE MOMENT

... INDER   BDR. W. BAWSTHORNE

... MERCHANT   A CLEVER ...

AND OTHER ARTISTES

SURPRISE ITEMS — COMMUNITY SINGING

ADMISSION FREE   (... GUEST)

A boyhood
venture into
ventriloquism.
Walter with
Henry and Peter.

A different kind
of lip service:
getting Gunner
Jimmy Turner
on the move...

'Legal Beaver' Lieutenant
Lawrence Firmin,
Courts Martial Officer at
Woolwich Barracks.

"Now we're
Kelly's eye"
Sergeant
Rourke, PT
instructor at
the 149th
Regiment.

BSM Hetherington, whose geniality
almost made new recruits feel very much
at home in the 149th Regiment, Hoylake.

3rd Corps staff
in Whitchurch,
Shropshire,
take a breather.

DE LA WARR PAVILION

BEXHILL

You have said Encore!

So here they are again—

THE

WHITE CLIFF
REVELS

FAMOUS ALL SOLDIER REVUE
with Original Cast in
AN ENTIRELY NEW SHOW

★

FRIDAY, 23rd FEBRUARY, 1945

at 2.45 and 7.15 p.m

BERT MATTHEWS
(Comedian)

WAL HUNTLEY
(Ventriloquist)

VIN CARDI
(The Revels' 'Bing')

RONNIE MASON
(Baritone)

THE CHOIR   ORCHESTRA
and Versatile Players

ALL PROCEEDS TO R.A. CHARITIES

Admission : 3/6 (Reserved), 2/6 and 1/6

Book your Seats NOW at The Pavilion and where advertised

Show devised and produced by 520 Coast Regiment R.A., Dover.

F. J. PARSONS LTD., BEXHILL

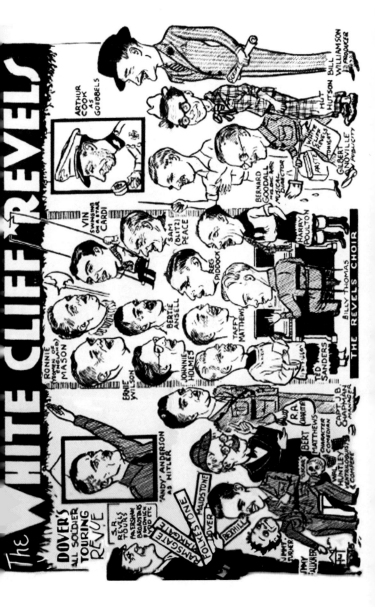

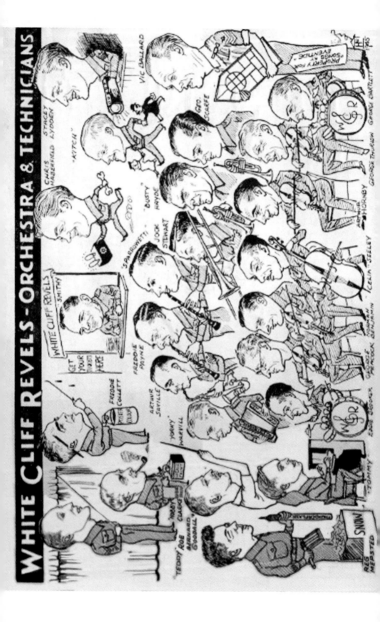

"You will put them through their paces on that march and not bring them back here in under an hour. Understood?"

"Yes. Sah."

"And when you bring them back I want to see them looking tired and weary. Understood?"

"Yes, Sah."

I wasn't too sure whether I had to wait for any further orders so I stood facing this tall commanding presence eyeing him slightly above his Sam Browne.

"What are yer waiting for, Sergeant? Get on with it..."

I did a smart about turn and was confronted with these massed ranks stretching away to what seemed like infinity.

"Att-ent-ion!" I heard myself roaring.

I, who had never taken a parade of even two soldiers, was now faced by enough troops to stage the Edinburgh Tattoo.

It was the moment to give it my best shot. "Left turn. By the left quick march. Left wheel. Left, right, left, right," and so we left the parade ground and headed down towards the town with me giving the performance of my life. So far, so good. I didn't hear anything from the RSM so I thought I had got away with it. So I had thus far. He, no doubt, was by now on his way for breakfast in the Mess. My mess was yet to come.

It began with the end of the first street we passed once we were beyond the depot. Almost imperceptibly the 'squad' began to get smaller as the first leavers disappeared up the street on the left. The next street on the right collected a few more who dodged off. And so on, street after street until I was left with a faithful few.

An hour, even with the faithful, was obviously going to take a lot of filling in and although the hemorrhage had slowed I was worried about how many more I could lose. I decided to chance my luck and return early before there was no one left.

SSH! THE S PLAN HESS-ITATION

SO I returned with a small residue of the massed ranks. My great fear was that the RSM would be there waiting for us. Not a sign.

He was by then no doubt relaxing after his plate of bacon and egg - even in wartime and rationing any Mess Sergeant, who had the responsibility for catering, also tended to have his own supply sources and would make sure the RSM was well looked after. So I shouted "Dismiss" and that was it.

I learned afterwards that the soldiers on parade were mostly old sweats from the British Army in India now called home; in short, time-serving regulars who no doubt had quickly rumbled they had a rookie in charge.

In the summer of 2008 I revisited the depot and stood alone on the parade ground where nearly 70 years before I had been all too well accompanied. The long line of buildings with its imposing façade is still MOD property and, so a spokesman told me, likely to remain so for the foreseeable future, though other parts of the depot have been converted to civilian use.

It is now a Grade I listed building. I'm glad it survived the post-war demolition mania. It is an important reminder of the glorious history of the Royal Artillery which even my involvement could not blemish.

I had arrived at Woolwich with the commendation from Captain Clarke-Smith to the Entertainment Officer on my entertaining ability as a vent and had soon been enrolled in the RA Depot Concert Party.

This was called Gunflashes and had received the blessing of the Commandant. 'Gunner Jimmy Turner' and I became an integral part of the show with me also involved in sketches.

Gunflashes was produced by Gunner Jack Cardew (later elevated for his efforts to Sergeant and made Manager of the Royal Artillery Theatre, at the front of the barracks) a 30-year-old actor and producer with experience of West End shows.

He became a great friend and mentor.

Jack had been an assistant to the well-known dance arranger Ralph Reader who later became producer of the wartime RAF Gang Shows. He had taken part in choreographing routines for the star of so many musicals, Jessie Matthews.

I had never met anyone like Jack Cardew before. He was so suave, confident, attractively craggy looking and very much a man of the world; and so talented. I was mesmerised by him.

He came from a background far removed from my own suburban upbringing and opened my eyes to life as lived in showbusiness on and off stage. Sexy, starry and seamy.

Much of the scenery and even some of the costumes for Gunflashes' productions were created out of materials salvaged from the damage caused by bombs on the barracks. The show proved so popular that the Royal Artillery Theatre was reopened and we now had the benefit for some of our shows of the Royal Artillery Revue Orchestra in the pit.

Cardew had created for himself a comfortable little flat which probably rivalled the accommodation of most of the officers. He had found a corner of the depot which seemed to have been forgotten and created his living quarters there.

Somehow he had managed to import a bed, settee, chairs and other furniture including a standard lamp, then a popular item in any sitting room. He walked through the depot carrying this one day without attracting anyone's attention.

It seems incredible that anything like this could happen. But the situation itself was incredible.

Only the permanent staff had any real control or status among a mass of all ranks who were on the move - and even the 'permanent' staff would be subject to constant change in this time of war.

There was, of course, also the nightly bombing which presented enormous difficulties. Some individual members of Gunflashes, including me with Jimmy, went down into the London tube stations being used as shelters to play to packed but often sleepy and exhausted audiences lying there on makeshift beds. Most seemed to appreciate the entertainment, but I think there were those who wished us to hell out of it so they could get a night's undisturbed rest instead of having to listen to Jimmy recite the alphabet while they were invited to "watch my lips."

Churchill had ordered that the anti-aircraft guns, almost useless because the German bombers were ungallantly flying above their range, should keep up the highest rate of fire possible to help maintain morale. It was a typically imaginative gesture by a skilful war leader, but it also had the effect of adding to the general din and smell of smoke and cordite. Was that huge bang one of our guns opening up or one of their bombs?

Many men in the barrack rooms, once used to house horses, would just put plugs in their ears and say "Goodnight all."

I envied them. I recall one night when I was playing darts with a fellow sergeant and all hell broke loose seemingly very close to us.

I could hear him saying "All you need is a treble nine and you're home and dry," as I threw a dart which didn't even hit the board.

My concern was acutely fixed on getting home in any condition. Was it courage or lack of imagination which induced his disregard to acute danger? Whatever, it was probably the most sensible attitude because there was nothing anyone could do in such a situation.

I slept on my table top desk in the Courts Martial Office and I think I can plead that my darts performance was not enhanced by the fact that the previous night I had been blown off the table and across the room as a window was blasted in.

Gunflashes was one of the first Army concert parties to include an ATS (Auxiliary Territorial Service later the WRAC) chorus and individual female artistes. One particularly bad night some of us had decided to take a breather in the trenches which had been dug on Woolwich Common to provide shelter.

It was there that I saw a bomb hit the building where I felt sure some of the girls were housed. In the flash which lit up the surrounding area all the debris could be seen quite clearly.

I was worried that it no doubt included body parts. An anxious check next morning brought the welcome news that none of our girls had been involved.

The national media - another term unknown in those days - had begun to give considerable attention to Gunflashes with stories and pictures in the press - one glossy magazine devoted a whole page of pictures to the show -and radio broadcasts in which I took part as a stand-up comic but without Jimmy.

The BBC had a policy that ventriloquism was a visual art and therefore had no place on the 'wireless'. Actually, they had already broadcast at least one vent, Arthur Prince as a Naval officer with his figure Jim dressed as a rating, I think it came from a variety performance at the Argyle Theatre, Birkenhead, which itself was to become a casualty of the war and reputedly had been the first theatre in England to 'go on the wireless'.

The irony was that vents became a popular feature on radio after the war. The breakthrough came through Edgar Bergen in America who had created a new style of act in which Charlie McCarthy's voice was in a higher pitch to make it distinctly different from his own.

The idea was copied by Peter Brough with Archie Andrews who became stars of the radio show Educating Archie. But the BBC policy of no vents on radio had some justification. Brough was a dreadful ventriloquist. When appearing on stage he had to hide his mouth with a large cigar and it became a joke in variety circles that he moved his lips more than Archie.

With the spread of television after the war the scope for ventriloquists became even greater and the stereotype of dummy was replaced by 'talking' animals - from dogs to ducks - and I even saw an act using a pair of shoes where the laces were tied in such a way as to look like two eyes and the upper part of the shoe parted from the sole to create the lips. I finally mustered 38 figures including a Chelsea pensioner and a blonde bombshell as well as a talking telephone and a cheeky bottle top who challenged my right to pour a drink.

But Jimmy Turner remained my best mate.

Vents like the brilliant technician Arthur Worsley who let

Charlie Brown do all the talking, Dennis Spicer with his novelty act, Ray Alan and Lord Charles and Keith Harris with Orville the duck were top-of-the-bill performers. But with the arrival of the Muppets and the ability of TV graphics to create a vast array of creatures of all kinds and shapes, ventriloquism seemed old fashioned and lost its popular appeal.

My memories of Woolwich include the night the Germans set London on fire and turned the sky such a bright red it was like dawn had broken; the moonlight coup by our fighters when a record number of German bombers were downed; and walking along a suburban street one evening with Jack Cardew and chatting about the show oblivious to the groups of wardens, police and civilians desperately trying to douse fires amid the rubble of what had once been houses.

Anybody who went through a night-after-night blitz in any city had such experiences. It was the way human beings continue to function on a day-to-day level in circumstances where there may never be a next day.

My service records made available to me by the MOD in connection with writing this book show that I had been posted to Woolwich to attend a clerks' course which would give me the necessary qualifications to become Sergeant (AC) Huntley - the 'AC' being artillery clerk, the reference to artillery being the nearest I ever got to being concerned with any gun much bigger than a rifle and then only on the firing range.

It was some time before I eventually took the clerks course presumably because I was in the show and once qualified liable to be posted and the Entertainments Officer or whoever wanted to retain me for the show. But the war came on the scene again and I had to move on.

We were now in June 1941. The previous month I had nipped down into the town to get my hair cut - not in preparation for the move because I had no idea it was coming. The barber decided that it was his duty to warn me that I was going bald - I was only 20 with a good head of hair - and that he sold a patent hair nourisher which, as far as he knew, was sold nowhere else in Woolwich.

I told him I'd leave my hair to fight on alone for its own future. He had as much chance of persuading young wartime soldiers to spend their beer money on a hair conditioner as the likelihood of Hitler winning the Nobel Peace Prize.

This interview took on a rather more significant aspect when my barber suddenly said: "What d'you think of the S plan?"

I'd no idea what he was talking about but out of the confused conversation that followed I gathered that Hitler's Deputy leader, Rudolph Hess, had landed in Scotland with a plan from Hitler to end the war.

When I got back to the depot I found hopes had been raised that the Germans were suing for peace. This highly unlikely expectation was short-lived.

The barber was right. It WAS an 'S plan' - Hess's own plan - which far from being endorsed by Hitler led to the deputy leader being stripped of every office he held right down to his membership of the Nazi party. He eventually died in Allied captivity, a forgotten old man.

The threat of invasion had led to an urgent stiffening of our defences and the expansion of gun positions around the coast - including up in Scotland where the sinking of the Royal Oak in Scapa Flow early in the war had sent out shockwaves.

I was transferred to Coast Branch RA and posted to Inchcolm Island in the Firth of Forth to run the office of 504 Coast Regiment.

Here followed the episode of the irascible Brigadier, who could roar like the lion that lay at his feet, the pen nib sergeant and the

Army tailor who was called upon to do a job on which his future depended. Let me elaborate.

All officers and senior NCOs arriving for service in this area had to undergo an interview with the Commander, Forth Defences - so on reaching Edinburgh I was summoned into the Brigadier's august presence. His sergeant clerk had been considerate enough to warn me: "He has a lion rug lying in front of his desk. Whatever you do, do NOT tread on it."

So on hearing the shout "Enter!" I moved smartly forward, my eyes fixed on the floor, snapped to attention well clear of the lion and saluted. There was a vocal eruption from across the desk:

"Eyes front, man, eyes front. What are yer looking at your boots for?" So much for the sergeant trying to be helpful.

Then, a meaningful pause, and: "Where the hell did you get that uniform! You look like a loose sack of potatoes leaning against a wall."

21 GUNNER SALUTE
WALTER COMES OF AGE

IT was only later that I tried to work out exactly how that description worked out. At that moment, I got the message that my appearance was short of appealing. "We've got to get you fitted out with something better than that."

In between these observations the Brigadier was obviously signing letters and every few seconds I saw that a pen went flying across the room. The sergeant clerk explained afterwards that part of his job was to scour the office once the Brigadier had left, pick up all the pens, fit them with new nibs and line them up on his desk like a row of cannons waiting to be fired again... "He likes new nibs every time," he said as though nothing could be more normal.

Within minutes of arriving at Inchcolm Island I was being measured for a new battledress.

The regimental tailor had been told that his attempt to make me look smart was to be viewed by the Brigadier so he had better make a good job of it. In fact, I was posted again before there was time for the further inspection. The tailor was probably even more relieved than I was.

There was a state of near panic in the Forth on any day that the Brigadier's launch was seen to be leaving Leith.

"Where was he heading? Which island?"

In case it was Inchcolm, the RSM would summon several working parties to spruce everywhere up, including removing seaweed from the jetty in case the Commandant should slip.

It seems hardly necessary to comment that there was not much chance of staging any entertainment here. Even if the general atmosphere had been more relaxed, apart from a few servicemen and the guns the only other inhabitant on the island was a mature lady who was custodian - if that is the correct description - of the ruins of an abbey. No chance of an ATS chorus and not much scope for enough talent from a small garrison to form a concert party.

The only entertainment in which I was involved, apart from doing a turn in the Sergeants' Mess, came with the visit of an ENSA (Entertainment National Service Association) troupe. ENSA was looked on with some contempt from young entertainers in the Services because it contained so many old pros well past their best. Even among the troops it became translated as Every Night Something Awful which was a rather sweeping condemnation because there were also some top line shows.

The troupe visiting Inchcolm heard that I was a vent and asked if I could do a spot to give them a break which I did with Jimmy who had accompanied me even there.

It could have been a bleak existence except we were all kept very busy. We got a 24-hour pass to Leith every fortnight and so on to Edinburgh where the Imperial Hotel had special low rates for Service personnel. I was invariably alone on leave with nothing much to do but join in the pub night life which was enlivened by the many Polish soldiers temporarily stationed in Scotland's capital.

I overslept one night at the Imperial, waking up to find my watch had stopped. I had no idea of the time and blithely came down to the dining room just before lunchtime to receive distinctly hostile looks from the staff when I asked what was on for breakfast. "Breakfast? Dinna yer know the time?" In fact I had no time for anything to eat but had to race to Leith with only minutes to spare to catch the boat back.

I spent my 21st birthday on Inchcolm. This was in the days when this particular birthday also conferred adulthood. I set up a drinks kitty in the Sergeants' Mess and continued to sup on as my companions headed off one after another. They included Royal Navy personnel who were stationed alongside us to identify any enemy ships trying to slip up the Forth.

Finally, in the late hours, there were just two of us left. My remaining guest was a portly Chief Petty Officer who met me pint for pint. Eventually he announced that he was 'bedwards' and walked out straight as a ramrod... I staggered to my feet and started my unsteady journey back to the Nissen hut which I had to myself.

It was along the cliff top and I had the presence of mind to realise that if I slipped down the side I would receive a Naval burial at sea without ever having joined that arm of the service.

So I crawled back on all fours and fell on to the bed and to sleep fully clothed. And that was how I 'came of age.'

I cannot claim it as a moment at which I can look back with pride, but it was of its time and age, especially mine.

Next stop was 510 Coast Regiment RA at the mining town of Blyth, Northumberland, in the September of 1941. Here again I had the blessing and even enthusiasm of the CO to get a concert party going. It took three months to get the show Rise and Shine on the road.

I was fortunate to have as co-producer Gunner Eric Thomas (stage name Eric King) who had been touring with his dance partner in a show called Going Gay; the word 'gay' did not have the connotation it acquired later after homosexuality had become legal.

It was straight concert party - no pun intended - with sketches rather than variety but we had three instrumentalists, enough to provide a small band and give the show a lift... I also did a Sunday show with Jimmy at the Grand Theatre, Byker.

My CO received a request from the Commandant of the RA Depot for me to return on loan for a special Gunflashes show so I headed back south again with Jimmy for a four-day 'attachment' which covered rehearsals as well as the show itself at the Royal Artillery Theatre.

There being no ATS available at Blyth I explored the possibility of recruiting local girls to form a chorus for Rise and Shine but I got nowhere with that one. There were problems of having civilians going in and out of the base in the middle of a war. So we carried on as we were.

I had a further indoctrination in how the Army works - and it was far removed from the admin procedures at which I was kept very busy between shows. The RSM took a nap every afternoon and used me as his cover. Straight after lunch in the Mess he would look in on the CO to report whatever he could think of and then retreat to his room for a nap.

He would say: "If the Colonel wants me, Sergeant, you know where I am... Give me a buzz."

Soon it came down to just a meaningful nod in my direction. But before he settled down on his bed he would walk past the CO's office shouting: "That man there. Move like a soldier. Head up, left, right, left, right" or "You there. Look at this mess here. Get it cleared up."

Any number of variations. In most cases, there was not a soul around except him. It was a well-rehearsed solo performance. The Colonel thought the world of him.

I also had further insight in to how army manoeuvres could be carried out in comfort.

One sergeant major who was handsome and good company specialised in the enticement of mature ladies. He had two widows in tow. One was the motherly type and the other the wealthy type who had been left well off by the recent death of her businessman husband. Neither had the slightest notion of the existence of the other.

He would announce to the motherly widow that he had to go on manoeuvres and she would lend him her car, give him a bottle of whisky to keep him warm out in the open and a box of sandwiches. He would stop en route and eat the sandwiches and then roll up at the house of the other widow to whom he presented the Scotch. After enjoying the good life over an amorous few days for which he had taken leave, the wealthy widow would say "One good turn deserves another" and give him a bottle of Scotch to take back with him.

In between "manoeuvres" he did find time to ring his wife - to tell her how desperately sorry he was that he just couldn't get any leave at the moment. He was in short, totally amoral and shameless. The remarkable thing was that he was also such a nice guy, a rare combination - to men, one of the boys and to women, irresistible. "If I can make three women happy, what's so wrong with that?" was his guiding tenet.

In the summer of 1942 I was posted as chief clerk of 550 Coast Regiment RA in Folkestone and from there to 520 regiment at Dover and the White Cliff Revels, a quite remarkable situation in the middle of a world war where more than 40 gunners left their guns, which were constantly in action, to put on greasepaint and tour the towns along England's south coast in an area known as Hellfire Corner.

I had heard of the Revels before but had never imagined I would become a member. There was at this time an organisation known as the Lord's Day Observance Society devoted to preserving the sanctity of the Sabbath as laid down in the 1780 Sunday Observance Act. Such variety shows as were able to take place under the law as it stood had the bizarre anomaly that they could not include a double act which was good news as far as I was concerned. Anyone talking to themselves like a ventriloquist did not count.

No doubt impressionists would also have been approved though I can't remember any well known acts of that type as happened in much later years when a whole show could be built around a skilled impersonator like Rory Bremner.

Anyway, for me this loophole meant I could do Sunday shows as 'foreigners' and I appeared several times with Jimmy at the Leas Cliff Hall in Folkestone.

The man behind the Lord's Day ban was a Mr Martin, dubbed by his opponents as 'Misery Martin'. Mr Martin stepped in when he heard that the White Cliff Revels were staging a show on a Sunday and it had to be called off.

The national press took the issue up on the side of the Revels and comedian Tommy Trinder stepped in to announce that he would stage a charity show to make up for any funds lost through the cancellation - the Revels' shows were all put on in aid of the Royal Artillery Benevolent Fund which helped to care for war widows and ex-soldiers in need of support.

The show was staged at the Royal Hippodrome in London and on a Sunday but within the law. It had a bill of famous artistes including Trinder himself, Tessie O'Shea, Derek Roy and Sonnie Hale. I don't think it provoked any reaction from the society which lost a lot of support.

I joined the Revels for the third edition of the revue, stayed through to the fifth and was also the compere. We played the 'big dates' like Dreamland, Margate, Westcliffe Theatre, Ramsgate, Globe Theatre, Deal, Garrison Theatre, Lydd, Leas Cliff Hall, Folkestone, De La Warr Pavilion, Bexhill, right down to the East Street Institute, Faversham. Prices of admission varied slightly according to the status of the place we were playing, but were around the 2s 6d reserved (12. 1/2p) to 1s 6d (7.1/2p) and 1s (5p), proceeds to the RA Benevolent Fund.

We played to American troops as well as our own, but mainly to the civilian population who had gone through so much with the bombing - and shelling for those still trying to live in the Folkestone/Dover area - and then had the terrifying ordeal of the 'doodlebug,' the Germans' V1 weapon and even many of the V2 rockets aimed at London which had fallen short and come down in Kent.

What I remember most about the V2 rockets - the development of which led eventually to putting man on the moon - was that you heard the huge explosion first then the whine of the V2 coming down afterwards.

DOODLE BUGS, GASMASKS AND
PINGS THAT GO PING IN THE NIGHT

IN the summer of 1944, my unit decided the war was going well enough to engage in some social activities with the population, more precisely the girls, in the surrounding areas.

So a dance was to be organised and our American friends now serving alongside us in providing AA (anti-aircraft) cover to the south coast were to join us as hosts.

Invitations went out and we awaited the arrival of the girls. A few, very few, turned up. It looked like being a huge flop with men left to dance with men!

"You want girls," said our transatlantic allies. "We'll get 'em for you."

And they sure did. They set out in trucks scouring the surrounding countryside and came back with literally truckfuls of girls.

It went off wonderfully well, but I wonder how many GI brides owed their new status to that night!

Overall we had a very good relationship with the Americans on our site. There was warm appreciation that they had finally come into the war and that would hasten the end. It was like an intake of oxygen to a war-weary nation.

But elsewhere there were incidents of clashes between our Tommies and their GIs - over girls, of course.

The GIs had everything going for them. Their uniforms were much smarter than ours, they had more money to spend and they had nylons and candies to give away. The arrival of talkies to our cinemas not many years before had brought Hollywood to our own front door. And in the eyes of the girls here was Hollywood in the flesh.

There was a bit of doggerel going the rounds which sums it all up. "You're oversexed, overpaid and over here," said our lads. And the response was "You're undersexed, underpaid and under Eisenhower."

As Churchill once put it we were two nations divided by a common language.

Earlier the rumours had been growing of 'Hitler's secret weapon' which was how the V1 came into our lives. I remember the first evening the doodle bugs came over. I had known they were coming because much Top Secret information had been circulated and I was considered one of those with "the need to know." Someone had to do the typing after all. The flying bombs were code named 'Divers' and we were ready for them.

We had Bofors AA guns ready to open up as soon as they appeared; and that first evening they began to fire as a stream of doodle-bugs came flying over. We later also had the American battery beside us with radar controlled AA guns and they scored a high rate of success.

Soldiers gathered on the cliff top and marvelled that these planes seemed to be totally oblivious to the AA fire. Even though the doodle-bugs were small, it was difficult at first sight to get a true perspective. "You've got to give these pilots credit" said one bombardier. I didn't know whether I was allowed to tell them the truth, but it soon dawned.

Sometimes our AA would hit one of the wings of a V1 enough to turn it round, and back it would head across the Channel.

Other times a direct hit would not explode the bomb but simply bring it down. A couple landed in the American area and there were a number of casualties. One V1 which came down in our area carried no explosive at all. It was full of propaganda pamphlets protesting at the "barbaric destruction of German towns."

The doodlebugs often arrived under the most unexpected situations. I was travelling on a train to London when the passengers suddenly became aware of the thump-thump-thump of a doodlebug above us and pulling down the window and looking upwards saw it was travelling right above the train.

There was considerable alarm that it might cut out and come down on the track just ahead of us. We waited for the dreaded sudden cut-out of the engine, but fortunately - for us, not someone else - it kept going and the route of the rail line caused the train to change direction.

On clear days from our vantage point on the cliff top we could see the V1s start their journey and follow them all the way across the Channel. Sometimes, the engine could cut out on approach to the cliffs and send everyone scuttling in all directions as we tried to guess where it would land...

What most intrigued me about the Americans was not just their highly efficient guns, but that the GIs never went anywhere except in their jeeps. They even went to 'the bogs' on four wheels. We walked everywhere, often in company when sanitary facilities were needed. Because it became a routine when someone felt the need to ask: "Anyone want to go to the bogs?" and someone would invariably say "Yeah, I'll come with you." And there was no ulterior motive involved. Just being pally.

As the regimental chief clerk, I was able to slip down to the local without the need of a pass. One evening I was sauntering down towards Dover when the Germans began a burst of shelling. I had not told anybody I was leaving HQ and the thought suddenly struck me that if instead of downing a pint a stray shell downed me no one would ever know just what had happened to me. They would probably think I had gone AWOL!

I had been told by someone who knew more about the mechanics involved than I did that our guns could not reach France, only the shipping lanes off the coast, whereas their guns could hit our port installations and defences. The battering taken by Dover was evidence that the latter was true.

But it struck me as a bit unfriendly of the French to build guns with such a long range, although, of course, they had no idea they would ever be used by the Germans.

By this time the Allies had pushed on following the D-Day landings and the Canadians were moving in behind the guns on the French coast. Eventually we heard they were very close and the rate of fire from across the Channel intensified.

We decided the German gunners were pounding the largely deserted town of Dover to use up as much ammunition as possible before they could fire no more. A few of us strolled out on to the cliff top to get a grandstand view of the finale - rather as one might appreciate a fireworks display. Suddenly, the range and direction of the firing changed and shells began to hit the cliff where we were - one coming very close. We vacated the area at a rate which almost beat the time it took for the earth thrown up to come down again! Shortly after we got the message from the Canadians that the gun positions had been taken and the Germans had surrendered.

The guns went quiet. 'Hellfire Corner' was at last over for Dover. This part of the South Coast was truly the nearest Britain came to having its own theatre of total war.

During all the shows I tried to keep an eye on the office I was supposed to be running. But it was mainly run by my Welsh 2i/c Bombardier Ivor Dallimore who sent me a round robin signed by himself and the other five clerks.

It read: "At a meeting of the staff held today, it was unanimously decided to approach you with a view to getting permission for the allocation of your army pay among the Boys who now have to do your work. It is not so much the money as the principle which is at stake."

The reference at the top of the paper was: Muggins 1/2/3/4/5/6. It was all a huge joke, of course. Who am I kidding? Thanks lads. I hope I took you all for a drink. While they did the work, we got the plaudits.

It was an all-male show with a full orchestra with musical arrangements by Gunner-Browning-Thomas and Craftsman Bernard Goodall, Mus.Bac.ARCO.

The ultimate accolade came from the Colonel Commandant of the Royal Artillery, General Sir Robert H Haining, KCB, DSO, who visited a show at the Leas Cliff Hall, Folkestone, and wrote: "It was an extremely finished and high-class performance and what struck me so forcibly was the keenness, enthusiasm and team spirit displayed by the performers. I don't wonder that the company has been such a success and I recognise to the full the amount of work it has entailed. This applies not only to all the performers but to the rest of the members of the regiment without whose co-operation it would, I think, have been impossible for the company to spare the amount of time that was obviously necessitated."

So, lads, you were appreciated after all - and at the highest level. But we're all well forgotten now.

In September 2007 I went back to Folkestone and Dover to research material for this book.

It came as a surprise even to the Kentish Express to hear about the Revels and they devoted a whole page to my story of the shows that went on through the shelling.

While stationed on the south coast I made some concessions to the military thread running almost imperceptibly through my life. I was by now well-versed in Army administration up to the demands of the role of regimental chief clerk and enjoying the status it conferred within the unit. I had also done some rifle firing on the ranges and if not a sharp shooter at least I managed to hit the target somewhere.

Further more, I had passed a course in small arms handling which included being able to strip and reassemble Bren and Sten guns. The tutor was a Cockney sergeant who had been an East End market trader and he had his own radical method of instruction.

He identified the various parts of the weapons by giving them names of parts of the human body, male and female, which were far from the ordinary medical terms used. There followed an explanation of what went with what. I don't know how he went on if he ever had to run a course for ATS girls.

It was decided that all ranks should visit the range at nearby Hythe and build up their skills at hitting bullseyes while wearing gas masks.

Presumably, some military phenomenon embedded in the system somewhere had suggested that the Germans might land under cover of gas. That would necessitate that they were wearing gas masks themselves which seemed an unlikely scenario.

But once the spectre had been raised it had to be exorcised.

So we were off to the ranges.

Doing anything with a gas mask on your head is difficult enough, particularly if, like me, you are also wearing spectacles in order to have any idea of what might constitute the target.

This had to be identified through the scratched and thick lenses of the mask misted up with your own breath now coming in heavy emissions.

As a sergeant I was particularly anxious that I should not emerge from this as the chief duffer of the occasion, which was a possibility I had to face, particularly under these conditions.

But I had no need to worry. There was in our ranks a Lancashire lad who had very big spectacles and thick lenses.

We lay down and took up our positions, put on our gas masks, and the order to fire was given by the sergeant major in charge.

Firing began and with each round there came a distinct 'PING PING PING,' not normally the sound expected of a bullet hitting a target but more likely a bullet hitting something made of stone.

"Stop firing! Stop firing!" came the desperate order. "Someone is hitting that tower. Take off your gasmasks and look long and hard at where the targets are."

We all did as we were ordered. It was good to breathe fresh air again.

"Now is everybody happy they know the target they're firing at?" No one demurred.

"Then we'll have another go. Gasmasks on and get in the firing position. Right, fire!"

PING PING PING.

"Stop firing. STOP FIRING!"

AN UNWANTED RIFLE IS
NO BARREL OF LAUGHS

THE sergeant major had quietly strolled along behind us and had spotted the culprit.

He was the Lancashire lad who had taken as his target the Martello tower beside the road along which traffic was passing to and fro and the odd pedestrian could be seen. An understandable mistake in the circumstances.

But it brought the sergeant-major to the instant point of admitting defeat. "That's enough for today," he said with the emphasis on the word "enough." He was obviously anxious to get us off the range before any peaceable citizen of Kent going about his orderly business should be mown down by friendly fire, to use that cosy but wholly unnerving term perpetrated in later hostilities.

"YOU," he said to the poor innocent lying skewed at an angle which bore no relationship to the direction of the targets, "are a bloody menace. You'd even be dangerous to the Jerries if they got here."

As troop concentrations built up around the south coast in preparation for D-Day and the opening up of the second front, a proscribed area was declared which included Folkestone and Dover. Soldiers from units stationed within the area could not travel outside the perimeter without a pass designating their destination. Ashford was the furthest we could go.

Someone probably destined to become one of Mensa's top performers realised that there were two Ashfords in the south of England - the one in Kent and one in Middlesex.

All it required was to get a pass to Ashford and write in 'Middlesex' after Ashford and that was enough to see you through to London and to satisfy any diligent operative of the Royal Military Police who sought to question the legitimacy of your presence. Ashford, Middlesex, became a popular tourism destination for soldiers who never actually got to visit the place.

There was one sergeant who had his own method of journeying at large armed with a device to satisfy any interrogation over his right to be at large - he carried a huge Bible. He was of foreign origin and something of a mystery to most of us because he rarely talked about his past or revealed any personal details.

It was generally rumoured that he had a tryst every Sunday with a local lady and would set off on a Sunday morning, his Bible under his arm, ready to meet any challenge with the assertion that he was a lay preacher at St Christopher's or whatever, and was already late for the service. He said the only time he was challenged the Military Policeman 'apologised before my godliness and wished me a good service.' This tactic enabled him to enjoy his leisure activities on a Sunday without having to seek a pass every week and possibly cause questions to be asked.

During the many shows of the White Cliff Revels it was inevitable that we had some problems - like the time our comedian, Bert Matthews, suddenly lost his way in his act and started it all over again repeating the same jokes. Bert, who was an old pro and always did well, had obviously lingered too long in the local before the show.

As the sergeant-producer, I dashed on, grabbed him by the arm and whispered "March off with me." I don't think he'd any idea what it was all about but he responded enthusiastically and we marched off in step like Guardsmen in the change-over at Buckingham Palace to huge applause from the audience. They obviously thought it was part of the act and a novel finale.

We considered incorporating it as a regular part of his routine, but you can't 'fake' a situation like that.

There was also a near crisis involving our magician who decided his act looked more impressive if he dressed up as a Chinese mandarin with a sinister thin moustache drooping down either side of his face.

The trouble came as he was standing in the wings waiting to go on and decided to lean over at the record player linked to the PA system to read the title of the piece being played as his introductory music. This, obviously, was difficult to do at the best of times and to do so just as he was about to go on was the worst of times. One end of his moustache became entangled in the machinery and he finished up with his head going round and round to avoid having his moustache painfully ripped off.

Meanwhile, the music continued to play him on and an empty stage awaited.

The problem was resolved by a quick thinking back stage technician who seized a pair of scissors and cut the mandarin free leaving him to rush on and face his public with a lopsided moustache.

From watching him from the wings I learned just how simple are some of the most baffling tricks - but having once briefly been a junior member of the Wirral Magical Society I will keep the secrets to myself.

The British Army had its own official entertainment unit, the Central Pool of Artistes, aka Stars in Battledress, to which I referred earlier. The War Office thinking was that if there was a crisis while a show was playing in the forward areas, the entertainers could revert to their soldier role and be used to strengthen the existing forces.

So it was decided to increase the number of SIB touring companies and my name was submitted as a possible member.

I auditioned at a hall in Harpenden before an officer from SIB. I was told later it was Captain George Black RA, a well-known producer of the London Palladium family and one of the founders of Stars in Battledress, who remained at the centre of the organisation and played a major role in its success.

I then waited for what I believed was the inevitable result - I would soon be a Star in Battledress. I passed the audition and received a letter from the Pool of Artistes confirming that an application had been made for my posting.

Then the war interfered again.

My posting was countermanded and instead I was sent to a training regiment at Larkhill on Salisbury Plain to be toughened up, trained as a counter-battery clerk and sent on an early draft to the Far East.

We were a group of sergeants and the idea was to instruct us in how to establish the position of enemy guns by plotting on a graph the direction of any sightings of gunfire reported by our own units. If the lines drawn from the angles of two or more sightings crossed, the point of the crossing was the Jap gun site.

Of, course it wasn't always as precise as that and there were classifications based on the strength of the information received. If positive enough it would be decided by a senior officer whether to call for an air strike or a barrage.

Looking back, it was a very primitive system, particularly as we'd now been at war for five years, but not quite down to the level of testing our ability to decide the direction of a noise in the dark. The point of this exercise was that the officers training us had all returned from fighting the Japs in the jungle and wanted to impress on us the skill of the enemy in creeping up to mount a surprise attack. So we had to be all ears.

The procedure for turning us into highly sensitive sound detectors went like this: we were split into pairs, one sergeant standing behind the other on whom he put a blindfold. The sergeant in front held a rifle at the ready. The officer then took several paces and struck a dustbin lid with an iron bar at which the blindfolded men had to point their rifles in the direction from which they thought the noise had come.

The outcome was hilarious. There was hardly anybody pointing at the dustbin lid and even the crest fallen officer, who up till then had been something of a martinet, couldn't help joining in the helpless laughter.

The rest of the training consisted of rifle drill, shooting on the range and assault courses, in the air and on the ground and sometimes in mid-air over pits with barbed wire in them to make descent unpleasant.

Reveille was 6am and all kit had to be laid out in the right order with a note from the QM to account for any item not there because it had been handed in for repair or renewal. We had to be absolutely beyond criticism on parade.

In a strange way I enjoyed it. There was a close camaraderie among us in our suffering and I was at a point of fitness I would never achieve again.

I did not go to the Far East with the rest. Instead I was called out and told I had been posted to "something called the CPA in London" and was to leave forthwith.

So I bade farewell to Larkhill and Salisbury Plain and all that went with it and set off for an entirely different style of life to a chorus of heartfelt farewells: "Lucky bugger."

Sergeant Bob summed it up: "I think I've seen everything now - someone taken off a draft for a war zone because he was a ventriloquist!" That got a big laugh.

Then he pondered on the implications of what he had said. "Hey, hang on," he said. "I think you should be coming with us as a ventriloquist, Wally.

"Then you could throw your voice around in the jungle and have the Japs firing at all the wrong places. That'd be better than bangs on a dustbin lid."

But the others did not need to practise drawing graphs or even trying to detect bangs on a dustbin lid much longer. Soon after they had finished the course and reached their destination the two atomic bombs had brought the Japanese to the peace table.

I left Larkhill looking smart enough to do duty at Buckingham Palace, fully blancoed and complete with kitbag and rifle.

My arrival at 10 Upper Grosvenor Street, London, caused consternation. There were two problems - first, I had to find some civilian accommodation because Upper Grosvenor Street, even in its faded elegance, was far from the usual British Army facilities. That was soon sorted. I knew just where I could go and be welcome. I would also get subsistence allowance on top of my army pay.

The second problem was more difficult to solve. What can one do with an unwanted rifle in the middle of the West End?

CSM Stanley Hall, who had welcomed me to the Central Pool of Artistes, said: "We have nowhere here to keep it. I think you'll have to go to the Guards' depot and see if they're willing to take it off you."

"Right, S'armajor" I replied. "Don't bother with that" he said. "We don't do that round here. I'm Stan. Glad to meet you, Wally."

Stan Hall was a leading make-up expert who, before the war, had been under contract to Sir Alexander Korda, the film pioneer.

I had only just stepped over the threshold and already I was entering the top echelon of the British entertainment industry though, because he was such a nice, unassuming guy, it was only later that I discovered Stanley Hall's background. He suggested that if I could turn up around nine to half past the following morning - minus the rifle - it could be decided which show I should join.

So I set off walking the streets of London in the midst of a world war with an unwanted rifle. At the Guards' depot there was even more consternation over the situation. "You should take it back to the unit you came from," said the duty sergeant.

I tried to explain that that was not possible and why I was asking him to take it off me. "What sort of artists are they in the army - war artists or something?" he muttered.

A young second lieutenant was summoned.

"Well, I can't see any reason why we shouldn't accept it," he said and started to walk off. Then he turned on his heels. "Make sure you put it down in the record book, sergeant, and the sergeant must accept a receipt for it."

So they gave me a receipt and I said another farewell - this time to my Lee Enfield.

ROLE CALL
AN ALL-STAR CAST

STARS in Battledress drew its artistes from across the regiments of the British Army and across the range of entertainment - from speciality acts like magicians and jugglers through to drama productions with 'straight' actors, who, in those days were considered a cut above variety performers.

Stars in Battledress was really a misnomer.

The title should have been Stars-to-be In Battledress because the bulk of the talent from which the companies were drawn had been amateurs or semi-pros who had blossomed under the increasing emphasis placed on the need for wartime entertainment.

There were some who were professionals before the war on the edge of stardom and some who became stars afterwards. So you get many names of artistes who at one time or another were with Stars in Battledress and became famous in the post-war years - among them Terry Thomas, Spike Milligan, Harry Secombe, Janet Brown (with her famous impersonation of Mrs Thatcher), Reg Varney (TV series On The Buses) Charlie Chester, Arthur Haynes, Ken Morris (radio show Stand Easy and the Charlie Chester Show), baritone Bruce Kent, comedian Norman Vaughan and singer Frederick Ferrari, both from Liverpool, Ken Platt ('I'm not stopping') and actors Richard Pascoe, Faith Brook and Michael Dennison in the drama productions. That is far from a comprehensive list.

Unfortunately there was not a great deal of socialising at Upper Grosvenor Street because we started on getting our shows together soon after arrival and went straight to our rehearsal rooms in the West End every day before we set off on tour.

The only celebrity I came into contact with was Sergeant Charlie Chester who was NCO I/c scriptwriting and provided a contribution to our show. It was 'other ranks'- the run-of-the-mill who lacked the King's Commission - who benefited most from their time with SIB - because it was thought the status of an officer would be demeaned if he became a variety act.

Officers could produce but not take part. The logic is understandable. It would have been acceptable for a major to play Widow Twankey in a regimental one night concert, but not to be employed, as such, as a full time professional Army entertainer!

The company to which I was 'drafted' was called Going Places. It consisted of eight men and two women - ATS girls, as they were known then before 18 became the age of adulthood. We were all unknowns and stayed that way as far as I know.

Because I was 'in' before any of the others I was the first due for demob. Had I gone the show was to be broken up. So what would have been unthinkable at one time happened. I stayed on in the Army for a few months longer than I was required to do.

By that time the war was over and what's a few months when you're having a good time?

Actually, those few months probably altered the course of my life.

I had just agreed to stay in when I had a letter from a London agency, Charles Tucker's Enterprises, inviting me to call in at their offices to discuss being in one of their shows about to go on tour. I had to explain that I was not immediately available.

By the time I was demobbed, the market was flooded and they had nothing to offer me. Under the law your previous employer had to re-instate you on demob so I went back into journalism.

Newly formed SIB companies did a tour of units around

London before setting out to far flung places. This way they could be honed into shape. It provided a wonderful showcase for the London agents, which was how, I was 'spotted.'

Those visits provided the entry into fulltime entertainment for many and we all gave our best when the whisper went round: "There's an agent in the audience tonight."

The company I joined was in the process of being put together. Going Places proved anything but an appropriate title.

I was the sergeant manager and was told we would be heading for France. We never got there; we were switched to Northern Ireland and never got beyond the UK.

As well as playing at Army bases we also visited the other Services. We played in RAF hangars, aboard warships and in Army and 'civilian' theatres. All the dates were one night stands.

One night we could have all the facilities of a huge garrison theatre and the next be playing in a canteen with the stage constructed from table tops.

We were invariably made honorary members of the Officers' Mess and royally entertained after the shows which never failed to be a success. It was a dizzy, wonderful life and we all felt like celebrities. Looking back across the decades I must be honest and admit we were probably not quite as good as we thought we were. We were playing to captive audiences who would welcome almost any relief from routine and we had, what Terry Wogan calls 'points of reference'. Those are factors you are able to share with your audience so you have an instant rapport.

For example, in my case in good time before the show I would find out the name of the most unpopular senior NCO (RSMs excepted) and any other aspects of life that 'bugged' the lower ranks. My script was written in such a way that I had left slots where local references could be slipped in. When playing to American troops I always used a reference to Private Sadsack who, I had been told, was the character in a newspaper comic strip back 'Stateside'.

The act had developed into a sketch where I depended very much on the remote control system designed and made for me by John Jones in Whitchurch. I sat at a desk dressed as an officer with Jimmy Turner before me on a charge and standing some distance away between two live escorts. I had a cable and a length of rubber tubing with which I worked him. The cable turned his head, and I had a bulb at the end of the tubing which worked his mouth.

The tube and cable were hidden by a wide mat and fed between the two escorts into Jimmy's back. All the escorts were required to do for the whole act was to stand in position, look fixedly to the front and not speak a word.

Normally the escorts were members of the show but if we changed the programme I had to recruit volunteers from the unit we were visiting. I always impressed upon the volunteer escorts that they must on no account move whatever happened.

One night I suddenly took it into my head to shout at Jimmy "One step forward," with the idea that he would shout back "You'd need a better remote control for me to do that."

Unfortunately, I must have made a convincing officer because one of the escorts did just that and stood on the cable and tubing under the mat.

Here I was in the middle of the act at a packed garrison theatre and unable to continue. So I stood up and walked over to berate Jimmy with anything that came into my head while glaring at the offending escort and between my lips repeating: "Get back, get back, you're on the mat." It was actually in rather more forceful language than that. Finally, he got the message and I returned to my desk relieved to find the cable and tubing connections still worked.

In the cross talk with Jimmy I had these prepared spots where I could use the important local references. Like I'd ask Jimmy what was his ambition in the Army and he'd reply "to be like Sergeant-Major Jones/Sergeant Smith," or whoever.

The mere use of the name would cause a roar because the audience would see it as ridicule and the victim couldn't complain, could he?

It was only as I was doing my research for this book that I discover a tattered piece of paper, which was the first sheet of the Central Pool of Artistes Part 1 Orders from Lieutenant-Colonel J A Lasbrey, dated May 9, 1946.

It read: 'A directive has been received from the War Office to the effect that in future skits at the expense of officers and sergeant-majors will be banned. During the war when officers and men have been serving together for long periods, and in many cases, in the happiest relationship, this type of joke was amusing and hurt nobody's feelings; but it has been noticed that young soldiers coming into the Army now and hearing such jokes in the early part of their training completely fail to understand the reason for these jokes and are often lead, through them, to breaches of discipline which causes trouble to the men concerned. All ranks are warned that a breach of this order will incur severe disciplinary action.'

There I go again failing to read Part 1 Orders - until some 60 years too late. I wonder what 'severe disciplinary action' I would have faced if I had been caught? Withdrawal of my allowance to cover greasepaint and other expenses?

The theatrical and the military worlds do not sit comfortably side by side. Training units were the bane of my life.

We may have been entertainers rather than soldiers, but we were dressed in uniform and to an RSM's eyes, we looked like soldiers; or more precisely, DIDN'T look enough like soldiers.

This caused constant problems. Like the time Private Hyde was told by an RSM "to get that hair cut at once and report back to me." Now, Private Hyde (A Voice And A Violin) did have an unusually good head of hair. It cascaded over the top of his battledress blouse and started making its way down his back.

The piece that always brought him the greatest applause was 'A Wandering Minstrel I' and he looked the part for that...

The problem here was that RSMs are not keen on having wandering minstrels wandering around their patch. On the other hand, wandering minstrels don't look like wandering minstrels with a short back and sides.

"What are you going to do about this, Wally?" was how the problem arrived with me. "Go and tell him we're nothing to do with him."

I somehow felt that approach might only exacerbate the situation! Even if it is put in the most diplomatic terms and the RSM is gifted with a broad sense of lateral understanding, most do not take happily to being told they're out of order on their own patch!

"We'll just ignore it," I said.

"It's all right for you saying that. I could be on a charge if I don't get my hair cut and report back to him."

We agreed a compromise. He would maintain a low profile for the rest of the day and if anything did develop he would say he had reported what had happened to me. It was a one night stand. We could make an early getaway the following morning.

So that's how I left it and we did a runner the next day. We never heard any more. Maybe the RSM had been told: "We have a troupe of poofters with us at the moment, Sir. He's probably one of those." That would be enough to cause any RSM to want to give up on life.

It was extremely disappointing that we had been switched

from France to Northern Ireland. Shows had been doing their bit all over the world - from Europe to the Middle East. But our visit to Ulster went well apart from our driver getting us lost in the Mountains of Mourne, which left an audience sitting in the theatre for two hours before the show started. It's very disconcerting to be greeted with boos and hisses the moment the curtain goes up.

Having our 'show clothes' enabled us to slip across the border as civilians and see what life was like in a country not involved in the war and with no rationing. In the restaurants we enjoyed meals to make British mouths water.

Mind you, even in Northern Ireland life was a lot better than on mainland Britain. Craftsman Doug Short spent all his available cash on buying enough cloth, available at an astonishingly low price, to make him at least one suit after demob. I was amazed at this.

His philosophy was simple: "If you have a good suit on your back you can go out into the world with confidence." I was content to rely on the demob suit I was going to be given free.

Two members of the cast, Private Peter Watts of the RAMC and Private Vic Thompson, a Yorkshire man who had found his way into the Leicesters, had experienced what entertaining in the forward areas could entail. They had been with General Ord Wingate's Chindits in India and Burma and had been in the Chindit Road Show. Soldier entertainers even popped up in the jungle.

Pete and Vic reached Imphal all set to do a show when the Japs laid heavy siege on the town. Instead of going before the footlights they went before the Japs to give them a show using rifles as props.

So they had been part of one of the crucial battles of the Second World War - to save India for the Empire of which it was 'the jewel in the crown.' Two years after the end of the Far East war the jewel had fallen out of the crown as India won independence. So many battles won in war, often with huge loss of life, are lost in the peace when force of arms is replaced by a wholly different set of values.

Though the government in the south of Ireland - after the war to become the Republic of Ireland - kept out of the war it did not stop young Irish men pouring over the border to join in the war, paradoxically, of course, to fight for the old enemy, England. They made up much of our audience in one unit we visited.

That night I had a visit just before the curtain went up.

"You the sergeant in charge?" said a slight figure in British Army uniform with a strong Irish accent. I owned up wondering what was coming. "Well you'd better not have any jokes about the Irish in the show, or you're in for trouble." I told him he needn't worry because we had no Irish material at all in the show.

Far from being pleased he expressed his displeasure in no uncertain terms: "You bloody English. You come to our country and then just ignore us." And he flounced off into the night. So wonderfully Irish. He was probably of less Celtic lineage than I am.

I still like the Irish. They're great company - as I found out later on press trips - and they have a legitimate grievance over their treatment in the past. I think at last it is beginning to die out in the new, forward-looking Ireland of the 21st century.

On one of those press visits, this time to report on the Republic's growing tourism industry, I was reminded of my first unit, the 149th Regiment Royal Horse Artillery that never got any horses. Apart from almost every pub we visited claiming to be Brendan Behan's favourite local because it served the best Guinness throughout Ireland, we also came across a village which had played a novel part in the fight against the British.

It was decided to form a cavalry unit but no local farmer would donate his horses.

So a meeting was held of the local commanders who solved the problem on the spot - everybody attending was lined up outside and declared to be foot cavalry.

The Irish tour saw the end of Stars in Battledress for all of us. We left Upper Grosvenor Street to go to our various places for demob with starry-eyed hopes for the future in a world which was going to be so much better.

My hero as I embarked on a newspaper career had been Arthur Christiansen the famous Wallasey-born editor of the Daily Express who changed the face of British journalism making it a great deal more exciting - or sensational his critics would argue.

Now I would be returning virtually to start all over again.

We also, of course, took with us our memories of Going Places and our two producers, the actor John Gabriel and Lieutenant Desmond Llwellyn, later to play Q in most of the Bond films.

CIVVIE
STREET
1945

CIVVIE STREET

I AM now 88. I went into the Army at 18 and came out at 25. Not a long period out of a lifetime yet the events of the war and its aftermath remain vividly in my mind - right back to those first troop concerts in the Parish Hall, Hoylake, staged by members of the 149th Regiment RHA, the unit that never got its horses but is still known to this day as the 'Hoylake Horse'.

Twenty years after VE Day, by which time I was features editor of the Liverpool Daily Post, I decided to try to see how much the post-war generation knew of the war. I set up a quiz paper under the title 20 Questions 20 Years After and carried out the survey through schools. The answer came back loud and clear: not a lot. And that was just 20 years later!

There was not even a clear grasp of who was fighting whom or how it had all started. To the question, "Who was Eisenhower?" one boy answered: "Hitler's favourite general."

Well, at least he knew he was a general.

We British have the admirable trait of being able to laugh at ourselves - a characteristic many nations lack. But I think it can go too far sometimes. TV shows like Dad's Army and It Ain't Half Hot Mum were gentle fun, but I felt 'Allo Allo' denigrated the enormous courage of the men and women agents who were parachuted into Occupied Europe knowing that if they were caught they faced certain torture by the Gestapo with almost certain death afterwards.

Some years ago I interviewed Odette Churchill, GC (later Hallowes) the French-born wife and mother who left the family life she had created in Britain to return to her native land as an agent. She was captured and tortured but survived, gravely ill.

She was nearly 70 when I met her, but she remained delightfully feminine and French, so unassuming and friendly it was like a chat with someone I had known for years. Yet I felt that quiet, strong character which had seen her through a terrifying ordeal.

Of all the people I interviewed over more than 50 years in newspaper journalism - including Prime Ministers and a wide range of other prime performers - this was the occasion I value the most. I feel we will always owe an immense debt to people like her and to the resistance fighters they supported as much as to our own front line service men and women and the many thousands of others who helped save our nation from becoming a colony of a German Nazi dictatorship.

My service records carry this 'testimonial' on demob: "Military Conduct: Exemplary. A very good and hard working NCO who has had active charge of a Stars in Battledress party on tour and has always carried out his duties most efficiently. He is also an artiste of originality." Signed: James A Lasbrey, Lieutenant-Colonel, Headquarters, Central Pool of Artistes.

Right to the end, there was this mixture of the military and the theatrical, with the theatrical coming out top. It well reflected my remarkable journey with Jimmy through the Second World War. Not the stuff of which heroes are made, but the way it all played out.

THE GREAT DISAPPEARING ACT

WITH demob Jimmy Turner went into retirement. He's still with me, but went gracefully into retirement because the act I needed as a semi pro was for a more intimate style of entertainment for clubs, dinners and children's shows.

I now worked under the name Clifton West with the slogan 'Novelty Ventriloquist - Watch His lips' because I was hoping to climb the editorial ladder and in those days it would not have appealed to the chairman of my company, the Liverpool Daily Post and Echo, to have had one of his executives going round with a case full of dolls.

I had figures of every sort and description, 40 altogether, including a tiny head bottle top that challenged me when I tried to pour myself a drink, a little pig that popped out of a hat as I was in the middle of doing a trick, a talking telephone, a glamorous girl doll and a cowboy. All were fairly small and easily transportable so I could carry several in a case and so vary my act.

The working men's clubs could be quite terrifying. You had to grab your audience the second you began your routine because you were competing with bar noise and chatter. It only subsided if it was decided by those in the room that you were worth watching - or at least given a try.

A place that club acts particularly feared was Haydock No. 2 - a miners' club in Lancashire. I turned up there one Sunday to be challenged at the door by a very substantially built bouncer.

"What dost thou want?" he said.

"I'm the paid artiste," I explained, using the recognised description which distinguished you from the volunteer amateurs you sometimes heard being booed off, usually while you were waiting to do your own bit.

Paid artiste also meant you would earn £1.30s (£1.50p) and sometimes be called upon to do three acts.

"A singer are yer?" asked the rotund shape studying me with curious eyes.

"No. I'm a ventriloquist."

"What the bloody hell's that?"

"I have dolls that talk," I said.

"Jesus. We've never had ought like that 'ere before."

It was not the sort of comment to lift my confidence already at zero. This was in the days when Sunday Night At The London Palladium with Bruce Forsythe, compering some of the nation's best acts, was drawing a mass audience to enjoy the comparatively new experience of television.

One club I visited had capitalised on this by having a huge screen which dropped down behind the stage to show muzzy black and white pictures.

I asked when I would be required to appear.

"Well, first we have bingo," said the social secretary. "Then we have the Palladium show and you follow that."

Children's shows could pose problems too, even though usually in a more restrained atmosphere. Again you had to grab your audience and work hard to hold its attention. I did this by asking at the outset for a boy or girl to come up and help me with the act. This involved using a series of different figures and tricks which had to be placed strictly in their order because I had to locate them quickly in order to avoid even the slightest pause, at which the audience would lose interest. It's interesting that the level of human concentration is very short at the start of life and returns to that condition as the end looms.

I was performing at the behest of a professor from Liverpool University who was giving a party for his grandchildren and their friends.

I asked as usual for a volunteer. It was always a case for a quick decision over which hand to acknowledge as belonging to the least likely child to be troublesome. This time I made a bad error. The result of my selection leapt up, put himself beside me and immediately began diving into my case and exhibiting its contents, thus destroying any surprise element.

Furthermore, this had the effect of mixing everything up, upsetting a small bottle of milk used in one of the tricks, over my precious figures and other items and rendering my act almost impossible. The response of clipping the offender over the ear not being available to me, I had the utmost difficulty of restraining him from further delving into my case while I jabbered on in an attempt to salvage some sort of performance.

Another time I was appearing before a large, young audience in a big hall. I worked hard and had the audience so attentive you could even hear one lad sneeze when two ladies walked in at the back of the audience carrying tubs of ice cream and, completely disregarding the fact that a performance was proceeding, one shouted out: "Any of you want an ice cream?"

Again, the show must go on against all the odds.

Dinners were top in status. But dinners, too, had their drawbacks, especially when entertaining the board of directors as I was booked to do one Wednesday evening. The dinner this time was for the board of directors of a shipping line.

In general if you appeal to the chairman you're well away. If the chairman laughs, everyone laughs. If the chairman claps, everyone puts their hands together.

This time there was an added hazard. I learned on the day of the dinner that the chairman of my newspaper, Sir Alick Jeans, was a member of the board and I just had to hope he would not be there. I think the shock of finding that Clifton West was aka Walter Huntley, his features editor, might have caused him some anguish and had fatal effects on my future with his firm which he ran extremely well but on rather paternalistic lines.

When I arrived at the hotel where the dinner was being held I was shown to a small room adjacent to the dining room where I could prepare myself for my act. I noted it had curtains rather than a door and you could pull these together and peer through a gap to suss out the whole scene.

It was also at ground level and had a window that led on to a yard. I decided that if I saw Sir Alick appear and take his place at the table, I would be out through that window, dolls and all, leaving the organiser of the event to think that he had mistakenly booked a vanishing act not a ventriloquist.

Sir Alick did not appear and the chairman laughed.

THE ART OF THE VENT

OVER the years many people have asked me what is the key to success as a ventriloquist. Is it just being able to talk without moving your lips?

The answer is that it is an essential requirement but just the starting point. You have to be able to smile, register facial expressions of interest, surprise or whatever and work your figure to bring it to life without showing any sign, physically or in your demeanour, that you are anything but completely relaxed.

Unless you can make your 'partner' real to yourself you have no chance of making him - I'll go for the traditional cheeky boy figure - look alive to anyone else.

There was a famous vent act called Coram and Jerry and Coram was reputed to go to his theatre dressing room early every evening before the show to have a 'chat' with Jerry. That could have just been good PR but it could well be true.

You must also give your figure a distinct character by the type of script you use, the way you manipulate him in bodily movements and reaction to what you are saying and in the use of the mechanical devices available to you - like being able to make him wink, move his eyes or raise his eyebrows.

Apart from all this, of course, you also have to remember your lines - and his!

How far can anyone throw their voice? The answer to that is hardly any further than any actor on any stage, because it is all an illusion. The timing of the movement of the lips has to coincide precisely with the words being used by the dummy - something else a ventriloquist has to get right.

The analogy is your television set. The sound is not, of course, coming from the lips of the person talking on your screen but from the loudspeaker. Your brain is so used to accepting the link between lip movement and speech that it is fooled - and fools you.

THE TRINITY MIRROR COLLECTION
New Books From Liverpool To Shake The World

Macca, The Saint and the Screen Goddess
Joe Riley
One journalist's lifetime of big interviews
£8.99

Liverpool: The Souvenir
An amazing city through your eyes
Daily Post
A showcase of Liverpool city, through a lens. The Flickr group,
created by the Daily Post have taken the opportunity to share
their images of Liverpool to provide a fascinating, beautiful
and at times poignant account of a year in the life of the city.
£4.99

Liverpool's Finest: Heroes of the Fire Brigade
Gavin F Bassie
A book of heroism that will fire the imagination
£14.99

Street Stars
Ray O'Brien
Star-studded guide to where the famous people of
Merseyside were born and the streets they lived in
£14.99

Spooky Liverpool II
Billy Roberts
Part two of Roberts' gripping collection
of the city's ghosts and ghouls
£8.99

Visit: www.merseyshop.com or call 0845 143 0001